The Palestinians

The Palestinians

**Other books in The Lucent Library of Conflict
in the Middle East series include:**

The Arab-Israeli Conflict
Human Rights in the Middle East
The Middle East: An Overview
U.S. Involvement in the Middle East: Inciting Conflict

THE LUCENT LIBRARY OF CONFLICT IN THE MIDDLE EAST

The Palestinians

By Anne Wallace Sharp

LUCENT BOOKS
An imprint of Thomson Gale, a part of The Thomson Corporation

THOMSON

━━━★━━━ ™

GALE

Detroit • New York • San Francisco • San Diego • New Haven, Conn. • Waterville, Maine • London • Munich

THOMSON

GALE

On cover: Palestinian women and children sit amidst the debris of their house, demolished by Israeli troops, in the Khan Younis refugee camp in the Gaza Strip.

Lauri Friedman, Series Editor

© 2005 Thomson Gale, a part of The Thomson Corporation.

Thomson and Star Logo are trademarks and Gale and Lucent Books are registered trademarks used herein under license.

For more information, contact
Lucent Books
27500 Drake Rd.
Farmington Hills, MI 48331-3535
Or you can visit our Internet site at http://www.gale.com

LIBRARY OF CONGRESS CATALOGING-IN-PUBLICATION DATA

Sharp, Anne Wallace.
    The Palestinians / by Anne Wallace Sharp.
        p. cm. — (Lucent library of conflict in the Middle East)
    Includes bibliographical references and index.
    ISBN 1-59018-493-9 (hardcover : alk. paper)
    1. Palestine—Juvenile literature. 2. Palestinian Arabs—Juvenile literature. I. Title.
II. Series.
    DS118.S4458 2004
    956.95'3—dc22
                                                        2004011084

55131264

Printed in the United States of America

CONTENTS

FOREWORD

On May 29, 2004, a group of Islamic terrorists attacked a housing compound in Khobar, Saudi Arabia, where hundreds of petroleum industry employees, many of them Westerners, lived. The terrorists ran through the complex, taking hostages and murdering people they considered infidels. At one point, they came across an Iraqi American engineer who was Muslim. As the helpless stranger stood frozen before them, the terrorists debated whether or not he deserved to die. "He's an American, we should shoot him," said one of the terrorists. "We don't shoot Muslims," responded another. The militants calmly discussed the predicament for several minutes and finally came to an agreement. "We are not going to shoot you," they told the terrorized man. After preaching to him about the righteousness of Islam, they continued their bloody spree.

The engineer's life was spared because the terrorists decided that his identity as a Muslim overrode all other factors that marked him as their enemy. Among the unfortunate twenty-two others killed that day were Swedes, Americans, Indians, and Filipinos whose identity as foreigners or Westerners or, as the terrorists proclaimed, "Zionists and crusaders," determined their fate. Although the Muslim engineer whose life was spared had far more in common with his murdered coworkers than with the terrorists, in the militants' eyes he was on their side.

The terrorist attacks in Khobar typify the conflict in the Middle East today, where fighting is often done along factionalist lines. Indeed, historically the peoples of the Middle East have been unified not by national identity but by intense loyalty to a tribe, ethnic group, and, above all, religious sect. For example, Iraq is home to Sunni Muslims, Shiite Muslims, Kurds, Turkomans, and Christian Assyrians who identify themselves by ethnic and religious affiliation first and as Iraqis second. When conflict erupts, ancient, sometimes obscure alliances determine whom they fight with and whom they fight against. Navigating this complex labyrinth of loyalties is key to understanding conflict in the Middle East, because these identities generate not only passionate allegiance to one's own group but also fanatic intolerance and fierce hatred of others.

Russian author Anton Chekhov once astutely noted, "Love, friendship, respect do not unite people as much as a common hatred for something." His words serve as a slogan for conflict in the Middle East, where religious belief and tribal allegiances perpetuate strong codes of honor and revenge, and hate is used to motivate people to join in a common cause. The methods of generating hatred in the Middle East are pervasive and overt. After Friday noon prayers, for example, imams in both Sunni and Shiite mosques deliver fiery sermons that inflame tensions between the sects that run high in nearly every Muslim country where the two groups coexist. With similar intent to incite hatred, Iranian satellite television programs broadcast forceful messages to Shiite Muslims across the Middle East, condemning certain groups as threats to Shiite values.

Perhaps some of the most astounding examples of people bonding in hatred are found in the Israeli-Palestinian conflict. In the Palestinian territories, men, women, and children are consistently taught to hate Israel, and even to die in the fight for Palestine. In spring 2004, the terrorist group Hamas went so far as to launch an online children's magazine that demonizes Israel and encourages youths to become suicide bombers. On the other hand, some sectors of Israeli society work hard to stereotype and degrade Palestinians in order to harden Israelis against the Palestinian cause. Is-

raeli journalist Barry Chamish, for example, dehumanizes Palestinians when he writes, "The Palestinians know nothing of the creation of beauty, engage in no serious scholarship, pass nothing of greatness down the ages. Their legacy is purely of destruction."

This type of propaganda inflames tensions in the Middle East, leading to a cycle of violence that has thus far proven impossible to break. Terrorist organizations send suicide bombers into Israeli cities to retaliate for Israeli assassinations of Palestinian leaders. The Israeli military, in response, leads incursions into Palestinian villages to demolish blocks upon blocks of homes, shops, and schools, further impoverishing an already desperate community. To avenge the destruction and death left in the wake of the incursions, Palestinians recruit more suicide bombers to launch themselves at civilian targets in Israeli cities. Neither side is willing to let a violent attack go unreciprocated, undermining nonviolent attempts to mediate the conflict, and the vicious cycle continues.

The books in the Lucent Library of Conflict in the Middle East help readers understand this embattled region of the world. Annotated bibliographies provide readers with ideas for further research, while fully documented primary and secondary source quotations enhance the text. Each book in the series explores a different facet of conflict in the Middle East; together they provide students with a wealth of information as well as launching points for further study and discussion.

Who Are the Palestinians?

The Palestinians are Arabs who trace their roots to the ancient Middle Eastern region of Philistia. Originally called the Philistines, they occupied the lands on the Mediterranean Sea in the area of what is now the state of Israel. This land, whose borders have never been clearly defined, was also called Palestine or the Holy Land because of its significance to Judaism, Christianity, and Islam. The region is today bordered by Egypt, Jordan, Lebanon, and Syria.

Controlled by the Israelites or Hebrews in ancient times, the land of Palestine eventually came under the control of many different rulers. As the gateway between East and West, the area frequently attracted waves of foreign invaders. In A.D. 636 Muslim Arabs took over Palestine, and the holy city of Jerusalem became a Muslim city.

Because of its important location, the region has been the site of numerous conflicts and wars. During the last half of the twentieth century, for example, the Palestinians and the Israelis have fought in five full wars and have been in a state of constant conflict. Former president Jimmy Carter sums up the region's past in the following way: "The history of . . . [Palestine] has been characterized by tremendous suffering and conflict among its people."[1]

The Palestinian Identity

Despite their connection to the ancient Philistines, the Palestinians had no concrete identity as a separate people until relatively recently. Before the establishment of the state of Israel in 1948, in fact, the term *Palestinian* was almost exclusively applied to the Jewish residents of the area. The Israelis have consistently argued that the Palestinian Arabs are not a separate people. They are also quick to point out that there is no language known as Palestinian, nor is there a distinctive Palestinian culture. Israeli sources elaborate: "There has never been a land known as Palestine, governed by Palestinians. Palestinians are Arabs, indistinguishable from Jordanians [or other Arabs]."[2]

Most historians and political analysts discount this perspective, but they agree that the concept of a Palestinian national identity is a recent one. Today, the Palestinians are the citizens of no country. They yearn for their own homeland and independence. "Palestine," writes *National Geographic* journalist Tad Szulc, "exists as a nation only in the imagination of six million Palestinians scattered throughout the Middle East, North Africa, Europe and the Americas."[3] They continue to work for international recognition of their

Palestinian Arabs have never had a sovereign homeland. One of their goals in the current struggle against Israel is to establish an independent Palestinian nation.

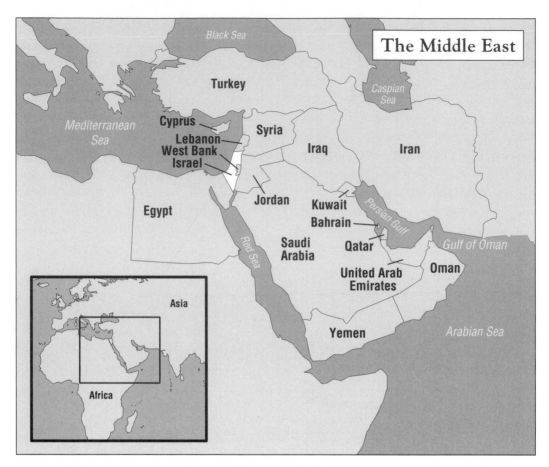

The Middle East

national identity as a people and their right to a nation of their own.

The Palestinians Today

A precise count of the number of Palestinians today is nearly impossible, although an estimated 6 to 7 million people identify themselves as Palestinian. Many of the original Palestinian refugees who were displaced in 1948 following Israeli independence have moved to other lands. Nearly 2 million reside in Jordan alone. Others have migrated to the United States and Europe. There are at least 4 million Palestinians still living in the West Bank, Gaza Strip, and Israel.

The Palestinians are a complex people. In some places, they are among the most literate, best-educated, and industrious Arabs in the Middle East. Historian David Lamb elaborates: "Most Palestinians are educated, middle-class, and economically successful. . . . Within their ranks are poets . . . millionaire traders . . . insurance brokers . . . importers . . . and professors at leading universities."[4] In other places, however, Palestinians experience extreme poverty and unemployment. The refugee camps where many of them live are places of squalor and desperation. Palestinians in the refugee camps account for 25 percent of the world's refugees and are, at present, the welfare wards of the United Nations.

Palestinians are both Muslim and Christian. (Christians make up about 12 percent of the total Palestinian population.) Toward the end of the twentieth century, more and more Palestinians began looking to their faith as a way to assert their identity and reclaim power over their own lives. Some of these people have embraced fundamentalism, a radical religious perspective. This has led them to become militants who turn to violence to achieve their nationalist goals. They sometimes recruit terrorists from among the many thousands of people who live in abject poverty in the refugee camps scattered throughout the region.

The conflict between the Israelis and the Palestinians during the twentieth century has given rise to hatred and distrust between the two peoples, which has been very difficult to diffuse. Each side claims the land, believing God gave the land to their ancestors to hold forever. All that both the Palestinians and the Israelis want, they say, is the ability to live in freedom in the land of their ancestors. No one, however, is completely confident that the two sides will ever achieve peace and reconciliation.

CHAPTER 1

Al-Nakba: The Catastrophe

At the opening of the twentieth century, the area of the world then known as Palestine was controlled by the Turks as part of the vast Ottoman Empire. Like other Middle Eastern areas at the time, Palestine was economically and politically underdeveloped because of long centuries of oppressive foreign rule. As a result, the Arabs who lived in Palestine had no political or social associations. This lack of organization impeded the Palestinian Arabs throughout the first half of the twentieth century as they tried to achieve independence.

World War I Comes to the Middle East

In Europe, the assassination of Austrian archduke Francis Ferdinand on June 28, 1914, precipitated an outbreak of hostilities that soon escalated into the first world war. While geographically remote from the early fighting, the Middle East was soon embroiled in the war as the European powers tried to elicit the help of the various Arab peoples. During the four-year war that followed, Great Britain and its allies, known as the Allied Forces, fought against Germany and its allies, known as the Axis Powers, which included the Turkish Ottoman Empire.

In order to defeat the Ottomans, Britain needed to establish bases in the Middle East to launch attacks on Turkey and to control the Mediterranean Sea. Since manpower was also needed, Britain turned to various Middle Eastern peoples seeking support for its war efforts. Large numbers of Arabs fought alongside the Allies during the war because they believed that if the Allies beat the Ottoman Empire, they would win their freedom.

Indeed, the British had promised the Arabs independence in a series of letters exchanged between Sir Henry McMahon, the British high commissioner in Cairo, Egypt, and Hussein Ibn Ali, an Arab leader in Mecca, Saudi Arabia. The letters, dated between July 14, 1915, and January 25, 1916, laid out the framework for future Arab states, including a Palestinian one. Summarizing the McMahon-Hussein letters, Palestinian historians write, "The British emphasized that the Arabs [including Palestinian Arabs] would be given their independence from the Ottoman Turks and that with British help after the war would establish their own . . . governments."[5] Despite this promise,

Arabs aided the British against the Ottoman Turks during World War I in exchange for a promise of independence at war's end.

the British had secretly decided long before the war ended to divide up the heartland of the Arab world between themselves and their allies. By 1922 Britain had taken control of Palestine.

The Balfour Declaration

At the same time the British were making pledges to the Arabs of Palestine, they also made promises to another group that wanted to establish a homeland in Palestine: Jews who were known as Zionists. By the end of the nineteenth century, the political movement known as Zionism had started in western Europe; it called for a Jewish homeland in Palestine based on biblical accounts of former Jewish occupation of that area. Zionism became very popular among European Jews during the early years of the twentieth century.

The Zionists received support for a homeland of their own in Palestine from British foreign secretary Arthur J. Balfour, who, on November 2, 1917, sent a letter to a London-based Zionist group. In it, he pledged British support for the establishment of a Jewish state in Palestine. This letter came to be known as the Balfour Declaration and was formally adopted as official British policy. The declaration stated:

British foreign secretary Arthur Balfour pledged England's support for a Jewish homeland in Palestine. This declaration upset Arabs who also had been promised sovereignty in the region.

His Majesty's Government views with favor the establishment in Palestine of a national home for the Jewish people, and will use their best endeavors to facilitate the achievement of this object, it being clearly understood that nothing shall be done which may prejudice the civil and religious rights of existing . . . communities in Palestine.[6]

With this support, Jews began immigrating to Palestine in large numbers.

A few years later, in 1922, Britain amended its stance on Palestine's becoming a Jewish state by publishing the first of what became known as the White Papers. In the first White Paper, the British government reassured the Arabs that it was not its intention to flood the Arabs' homeland with Jewish immigrants. Furthermore, the British promised that no decision on the future of Palestine would be made without the Arabs' approval.

This latter directive, however, was in direct opposition to the earlier promises made to the Zionists. By making these conflicting agreements, Britain had promised both the Zionists and the Arabs they could each establish their homeland in Palestine. In doing so, Britain had inadvertently created a near-impossible situation in Palestine. It became clear that sometime in the future the British government would need to decisively take one side over the other. For the immediate future, however, the British put off any decision and treated Palestine as a British colony.

Arabs Sell Their Land

After the League of Nations approved the Balfour Declaration in 1922, Britain began to rule Palestine under what was known as a mandate system, which meant that British military and colonial administrators controlled the land. The British hired a few leading Palestinian Arabs to fill various administrative positions but retained firm control of Palestine's economy and politics. Technically, this system was meant to be temporary; the long-range goal was to prepare Palestine for independence.

At the time the mandate began, the Arab population of Palestine was still suffering from the long years of oppressive rule by the Ottomans. Over 25 percent of the Arab population lived in poverty, barely able to provide for their basic needs. A series of natural disasters, including locusts, droughts, and an earthquake, made the situation worse. In the 1930s these conditions led to the Arab peasants' inability to pay taxes to the British government or meet their mortgage payments to absentee Arab landlords. Deeply in debt, thousands of Palestinian Arab farmers were forced to sell off their lands.

Most of this land was purchased by hundreds of thousands of Jewish immigrants arriving from Europe. Many of them came to fulfill the Zionist dream of returning to their biblical homeland and to flee an increasingly anti-Jewish Europe. Nearly 65 percent of all the land the Jews acquired during this period was purchased from the Arabs. Although they were in debt and needed the money, the Palestinian Arabs

Jewish settlers arriving in Palestine bought up land from Arabs who had been financially ruined by World War I and subsequent natural disasters.

greatly resented that they had to sell their land to the newcomers, who they saw as a threat to Arab dominance of the region.

Tensions Increase

As a result of this immigration, between the years 1931 and 1935 the Jewish population in Palestine doubled. Concerned about the growing domination of Jewish business and industry, a loose coalition of groups formed the Higher Arab Committee and called for a national strike. Arab workers walked off their jobs with British and Jewish companies, causing a virtual standstill of the colonial economy in Palestine. In addition, the committee urged Palestinian Arabs to boycott all Jewish and British products and goods.

The committee also demanded that the British colonial government put a stop to Jewish immigration, end further land sales to Jews, and establish a Palestinian Arab government. These demands were all based on Arab fears that, in time, their homeland might be taken over by the Jewish immigrants and become the political domain of the Zionists. This fear was quite realistic, as historian Michael J. Cohen explains: "By 1936, . . . the economic, industrial, and military foundations of the future Jewish state had been laid."[7]

These tensions soon gave way to violence on both sides. In April 1936 an Arab attack on a Jewish bus led to a series of incidents that soon escalated into nationwide disturbances. As riots and violent confrontations increased, the mandate system began to break down. Seeing violence as a way to force the British to approve Arab independence, militant and radical groups started to appear among Palestinian Arabs. These groups led attacks against the British and the Zionists, killing hundreds of Jewish immigrants and British colonial officials in bomb blasts, sniper activity, and acts of sabotage. At the same time, Zionist militant groups such as the Haganah and the terrorist group Irgun also emerged. These two groups began raiding Arab villages and planting bombs, killing hundreds of people. Thousands of Arabs and Jews were killed during this period of civil unrest.

The Partition of Palestine

By the end of World War II in 1945, the British still were unable to decide how to settle the question of Jewish or Arab independence. They therefore turned the issue of Palestine over to the newly

British Policy Is Reversed

The violence in Palestine during the 1930s, along with the strong probability of another European war, led the British to reconsider their policy in the Middle East. Britain decided to abandon its commitment to the Zionists and, instead, support the Arabs' goal of independence. Toward that end, the British government issued a 1939 White Paper that called for the establishment of a Palestinian state within ten years. Great Britain announced that Palestinian administrators would begin to take over the government as soon as peace and order were restored.

The British government also announced its intention to limit Jewish immigration and allow only ten thousand Jewish immigrants into the region during the next five years, and then none at all after that without Arab approval. The timing of this restriction devastated the Zionists. By 1939 news had begun to spread about Nazi dictator Adolf Hitler's plan to exterminate the Jewish population of Europe. Hundreds of thousands of Jewish citizens had been arrested and sent to concentration camps, where they were executed. European Jews, therefore, were desperately trying to escape Europe by seeking refuge in Palestine. With the new immigration restrictions in place, however, the Jewish refugees had nowhere to go. This so angered the Zionists that they began to organize an army to fight the British and to achieve an independent Jewish state.

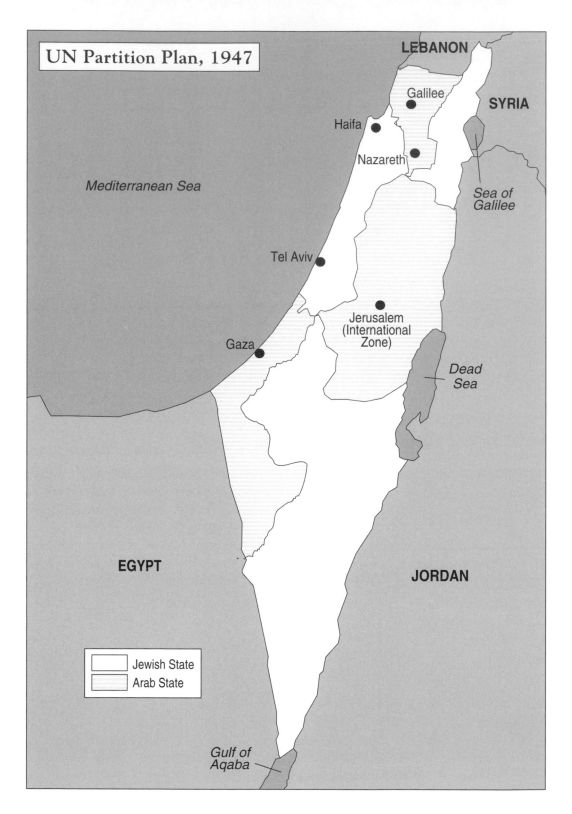

UN Partition Plan, 1947

LEBANON

Galilee

SYRIA

Haifa

Nazareth

Mediterranean Sea

Sea of
Galilee

Tel Aviv

Jerusalem
(International
Zone)

Gaza

Dead
Sea

EGYPT

JORDAN

Jewish State
Arab State

Gulf of
Aqaba

formed United Nations (UN). Historian Karen Armstrong explains the rationale for this move: "By 1947, the British officials in Palestine were demoralized, exasperated, and frustrated by the attempt to implement an impossible policy."[8]

The United Nations was thus given the task of determining the future of Palestine. In debating the issue, the United Nations decided that dividing Palestine was the only way to end the violence while still providing each side with a homeland. It therefore developed a partition plan that divided the land between the two competing groups. The United Nations decreed that the Zionists would receive 55 percent of the land, with the remaining 45 percent going to the Arabs. The Zionists accepted the partition. The Arabs, however, believed that the whole of Palestine was rightly theirs based on their long residence in the region. As historian Helena Cobban writes, "The Arab Palestinians, seeing the United Nations [partition] proposal as seeking to divide the land which they still claimed as theirs, turned it down."[9]

Despite Arab opposition, the UN General Assembly voted thirty-three to thirteen on November 29, 1947, to go ahead with the partition. The UN Resolution on the Partition of Palestine stated, "Independent Arab and Jewish states . . . shall come into existence in Palestine."[10]

War Is Inevitable

Despite the vote, the Arabs remained determined to prevent the Zionists from taking control of Palestine. As a result,

fierce fighting broke out between the two groups. Fighting also broke out between the British and the Zionists as the Zionists tried to get the British to leave the region so a Jewish state could be declared. To this end, Zionist militants killed nearly four hundred British civilians. In the late 1940s the terrorist group Irgun, for instance, under the leadership of future Israeli prime minister Menachem Begin, blew up an entire wing of the King David Hotel, killing ninety Arabs, Brits, and Jews.

As partition loomed, the violence increased and civil war became inevitable in Palestine. Each side believed that history supported its claim to Palestine; neither side would settle for anything less. Historian Cohen summarizes: "The determination of both Jews and Arabs to fight for what each considered inviolable rights ruled out all prospects of compromise."[11]

As the British pulled out of Palestine, the Zionists moved forward with their plans to establish a Jewish state. After decisive military victories against the fleeing British and the Arabs, on May 14, 1948, Zionist leader David Ben-Gurion proclaimed the establishment of a Jewish state called Israel.

This announcement of Jewish statehood led several neighboring Arab countries, including Egypt, Syria, Lebanon, and Jordan, to immediately declare war on Israel. Most historians agree that these Arab nations invaded Israel not out of any particular concern for the Arab inhabitants of Palestine but rather because of concern for their own borders. These governments were worried

The Role of the Holocaust in the Partition of Palestine

The world was horrified to learn about the murder of 6 million European Jews by the Nazis in what became known as the Holocaust. While rumors about the concentration camps and Jewish deaths had spread during the war, no one anticipated the conditions the prisoners were forced to endure and the massive number of deaths that occurred. The world was outraged when it learned that Jewish prisoners had been executed in gas chambers and subjected to deplorable prison conditions and torture. After watching the thousands of near-skeletal men, women, and children emerge from the camps, world sympathy for the survivors of the Holocaust surged.

This overwhelming sympathy led many world leaders to press the United Nations to act quickly on behalf of the Jewish survivors. Seeking to provide a safe haven for the surviving Jewish population, the United Nations ultimately called for the partition of Palestine and the creation of the state of Israel to become a homeland for the Jewish people.

As the horrors of the Holocaust became known, much of the international community felt that surviving European Jews deserved a safe homeland in the Middle East.

that Israel might invade their countries and take control of land they occupied along the newly established Israeli border. While outnumbered by the Arabs, the Israelis were far better organized, and their army, the Israeli Defense Force (IDF) achieved victory after victory. On the eve of the 1948 war, the Palestinian Arabs had occupied nearly 90 percent of the country, but at war's end Israel held over two-thirds of what had been alloted to become a Palestinian state.

The Arabs Flee

During the war of independence, the Israelis began implementing a detailed strategy for dealing with the Arabs of Palestine. This plan called for the expulsion of the Arab population living within the borders of the new state. Hoping to avoid lengthy and costly military campaigns, the Israelis used a variety of fear tactics to compel the Arabs to leave the region.

One particularly effective method involved spreading rumors and causing fear about disease epidemics. Loudspeakers mounted on Israeli jeeps and tanks blared warnings of smallpox or plague outbreaks to villagers, claiming such epidemics were occurring in nearby villages. Not able to verify the accuracy of these reports and fearing death from these very contagious diseases, hundreds of Palestinian Arabs fled their homes and villages.

After the British pulled out of the Middle East, Jewish forces attacked Palestinian settlements to drive the Arabs out of the region.

Loudspeaker vans also warned that anyone remaining in their homes would be summarily executed. One Palestinian Arab remembered such a warning: "Around midday the loudspeakers in the mosque announced that everyone in the village should come to the mosque or risk being shot."[12] Arab parents were also told that their children would be kidnapped or killed. Pets and livestock were destroyed, food supplies were cut off, businesses were destroyed, and entire villages were isolated. Palestinian Arabs were also ordered to walk as fast as they could toward the Jordanian border, which was many miles away. Israeli troops marched alongside the Arabs, prodding those who moved slowly with their bayonets and rifles.

These kinds of tactics instilled terror in the Arab populace, which saw no other option than to flee. "There is now irrefutable evidence," explains researcher Jerome Slater, "that most of the Palestinians who became refugees from Israel in the 1947–1949 period did so because they were either forcibly expelled or fled as a result of Israeli psychological warfare, economic pressure, artillery bombardments, terrorism, and massacres."[13]

"Bullets Glittered and Screamed in the Air"

Terrified by the advancing Israeli army and Haganah militants, entire communities left their villages prior to the arrival of soldiers and sought refuge in neighboring villages or in the nearby desert. Mohammed Masad, who was nine years old when the Israeli army attacked his village of Zeita, recalls his family's experience: "At nightfall we would huddle in the living room, lights off, and only a candle burning, to talk in whispers and listen to the incessant shooting ripping the quietness of the night."[14] Masad's family eventually fled

Why the Palestinians Failed to Achieve Independence

The Palestinian Arabs failed to achieve independence for a variety of reasons. Perhaps the most important reason was their misunderstanding of Western diplomacy. Instead of agreeing to the UN partition, which at least guaranteed them part of Palestine, the Arabs refused to consider compromise. By rejecting anything less than the whole of Palestine, the Arabs believed they would eventually force the West to realize the inequity of the loss of their homeland. Their strategy failed.

The Palestinian Arabs also failed because they were less organized than the Zionists. Politically, they were unable to speak with a unified voice in their negotiations with the UN. They also lacked an organized military force, and so they were unable to mount a sustained resistance against the tightly organized Israeli Defense Force. As a result of all these factors, the Palestinian Arabs did not secure independence.

Arab refugees escape fighting in the Galilee region of what is now Israel. Many Palestinians sought refuge in Jordan, Lebanon, Egypt, and Syria.

along with their neighbors to the nearby desert, where they lived in caves and crude shelters. Thousands of Arabs struggled to survive during cold desert nights while listening to the sound of gunfire in the distance. Many of these families lived in these remote desert wildernesses for more than a year before relocating to various refugee camps.

Mohammad Zahaykeh, a journalist who now lives in East Jerusalem, was a child in 1949 when the Israeli army in-

vaded his village. He spoke to writer Laurel Holliday about his experiences:

Our house was in the zone of fire. I was picked up by one of my family's relatives . . . who put me on his shoulders and swiftly evacuated me and the rest of my family while bullets glittered and screamed in the air and fell on the ground near our feet. . . . Fear filled my young heart as we crawled on all fours like animals to avoid gunshots.[15]

Entire Arab villages were abandoned as the Israeli army moved in. What property was left behind was confiscated by Jewish settlers.

Zahaykeh's father was killed because he refused to leave their home.

Thousands of Arabs were killed as the Israeli army advanced through hundreds of villages and communities. One of the most infamous incidents occurred at the Arab village of Deir Yassin. Jamil Ahmed, a Palestinian Arab, lived on the edge of the village and saw what occurred. In an interview with historian David K. Shipler, Ahmed reported, "I saw many friends killed. They [the Israelis] would enter the houses and throw bombs. I saw prisoners who were butchered. . . . They took them as prisoners . . . and took them to the end of the road . . . and sprayed them with gunfire."[16] More than 250 Palestinian men, women, and children were killed during this attack.

Al-Nakba

By the end of 1949, more than 1 million Palestinian Arabs had been forced to flee the region; barely 160,000 Palestinians remained in Israel. The Palestinian Arabs called this expulsion al-Nakba, "the Catastrophe." While Jews around the world celebrated the founding of Israel, the Arabs mourned it. They had been forced into exile and had no land to call their own. The land that had been awarded to them by the partition plan had not only been acquired by Israel in the fighting; it had also been snatched up by neighboring Arab countries. For example, both Jordan and Egypt seized remaining Palestinian territory for themselves, disregarding Palestinian desires for an independent state.

Wadad Saba witnessed al-Nakba firsthand before immigrating to the United States when she was twenty-one. Five decades later, she remained passionate about what happened in 1948 and 1949. "Palestine was literally stolen from me and my countrymen and renamed Israel in 1948."[17]

CHAPTER 2

The Growth of Palestinian Nationalism

After the creation of Israel and their expulsion from their former homeland, the Palestinian Arabs had no country to call their own. No sooner had they fled their homes and villages than the new state of Israel made their exodus permanent. Israeli troops confiscated property and established Jewish settlements in former Arab villages. Entire towns were bulldozed to the ground, and roadblocks were established throughout the state of Israel. Thousands of Arabs were stopped and turned back from trying to return to their homes. In this way, the Arabs became refugees and were forced to settle in makeshift camps around the region. United by their experience during al-Nakba, the Palestinian Arabs became a determined people with common goals: to return to their homeland and to create a Palestinian state.

The Refugees

The 1948–1949 war left nearly a million Palestinian Arabs homeless, many of whom had left villages and homes where they had lived for many generations. Most of these refugees settled in Jordan, Syria, Lebanon, and Egypt, where they found little acceptance among the societies of other Arab countries. Emanuel A. Winston, a Middle Eastern analyst, describes the situation: "The Arab refugees who had migrated to various Arab nations were . . . regarded not as Arab brothers but as unwelcome migrants who were not to be trusted."[18] The refugees, rather than being assimilated into other Arab societies, remained with their own people and settled in primitive camps along the borders of their former homeland.

The initial refugee camps were set up rather spontaneously. Families who

Although resettled in Arab countries bordering Israel, Palestinian refugees clustered into camps and remained isolated from the native populations.

had traveled together established makeshift homes with whatever materials they could scavenge from the countryside. As other Arabs joined them, villages or camps were formed. In the beginning, most of these camps were tent cities located near streams and other waterways.

The United Nations stepped in almost immediately and sent food, medical supplies, and building materials to the camps. A special organization, the UN Relief and Works Administration, was set up to deal with the growing number of refugees. UN volunteers arrived in the area to distribute food and to help the refugees build homes. Cement-block houses soon replaced the tent cities.

"Cinder Blocks and Metal Roofs"

Even with roofs over their heads, however, little comfort was found in the camps. Despite UN aid, most of the refugees lived with extreme poverty, lack of sanitation, hunger, and desperation. Remaining dependent on the welfare provided by international organizations was also disheartening and frustrating. The Palestinian Arabs yearned for the homes they had left behind. Palestinian Alexandra Avakian says of the refugees: "Grandparents in every refugee camp . . . remember exactly where they came from before 1948. They remember their village. They talk about the well and the orchards, and how beautiful their home was. And now they're living in these thrown-together shacks made of cinder

blocks and metal roofs, and often don't have running water, and the sewage is right outside the door."[19]

Many Arabs had no land or possessions in the refugee camps. Palestinian Ramzy Baroud describes his mother's life in the camps: "They [the Israelis] invaded her village and drove everyone out at gunpoint. . . . For the rest of her life, she would live in a lowly camp, riddled with disease, surrounded by barbed wire, filled with despair. Here she would grow up, marry, become a mother . . . and here in this camp, her children would watch her die."[20]

Filled with resentment against Israel, their hopes of an independent Palestine shattered, the Arab refugees nurtured dreams of one day returning to their land. It was in these camps that the hope for independence germinated into the creation of a number of groups that would lead the Palestinian Arabs forward into the latter half of the twentieth century. As the Palestinian Arabs began to search for a way to regain their homeland, a nationalist movement emerged.

The Beginning of Palestinian Nationalism

Prior to the establishment of the state of Israel in 1948, the Arabs of Palestine had never identified themselves as *Palestinians*. Rather, they were often linked to other Arab countries, such as Syria and Egypt, and referred to themselves simply as *Arab*. In the ten years following their exile from Palestine, however, the sense of being *Palestinian* and being a separate and distinct people began to emerge in the refugee camps.

For the Palestinians, the shared events of 1948 had created a collective consciousness that centered on a common enemy: Israel. Political analyst Adina Friedman elaborates: "The Nakba thus came ultimately to serve as one of the most important aspects of Palestinian identity and a source of shared belief and values."[21] It was, ironically, the Israelis—through their forced expulsion of the Palestinians, known as al-Nakba—who provided the Palestinians with their main unifying cause.

As a result of this new sense of identity, several nationalistic movements emerged in the late 1950s and early 1960s. One such group was the Palestine Liberation Organization (PLO), a group started by President Gamal Abdel Nasser of Egypt, who was, at that time, the most powerful Arab leader in the Middle East. His primary motivation in backing the Palestinian cause was his wish to further consolidate his own power at the expense of Israel. Nasser, like other Arab leaders, felt threatened by Israel's growing political and military presence in the Middle East. Because of this, Nasser readily embraced the Palestinians, hoping to enlist them in his fight against Israel.

In 1964 the PLO set forth its founding resolutions and principles. Its primary goals included the liberation of Palestine and the destruction of the state of Israel. The group's charter also condemned Zionism and vowed to work toward independence for the Palestinian people. During the first few years of its existence, the PLO was largely dependent on, and run by, President Nasser.

Israel Blames the Arab Nations for the Refugee Situation

While the Palestinians blame Israel for their refugee status, the Israelis give a very different explanation for the situation. Citing Arab hatred of the Jewish state, the Israelis argue that the Arab states used the refugee situation to turn world opinion against Israel. Ralph Galloway, a former UN committee member, explained this idea in 1958. His comments appear in "Refugees" in *Peace Encyclopedia*. "The Arab states do not want to solve the refugee problem. They want to keep it as an open sore, an affront to the United Nations and as a weapon against Israel."

Israel is quick to point out that many of the refugees who remained in Israel were treated more humanely than those who settled in Arab territory in the camps. Furthermore, Israeli leaders say the Arab governments that sheltered the refugees were, at the time, financially capable of improving camp conditions but often chose not to do so for political reasons. These reasons, the Israelis contend, include the Arab need to portray the refugees as the victims of Israeli aggression.

President Gamal Abdel Nasser of Egypt supported Palestinian nationalism because he feared Israel's strength in the Middle East.

Al-Fatah and the Fedayeen

While the PLO grew and attracted supporters, Syria began building another Palestinian organization. Syria, like Egypt, felt threatened by the Israelis and hoped to use the Palestinians to strengthen its own position in the Middle East. Syrian intelligence agents scoured the refugee camps looking for recruits who could be trained in guerrilla warfare to fight Israel. One of those recruited was a young man named Yasir Arafat, a Palestinian engineer who was dedicated to the cause of Palestinian independence. He had formed his own group, which became known as the Movement for the Liberation of Palestine. This group is better known as al-Fatah, an Arabic word meaning "Victory" or "Conquest."

One of the first moves by al-Fatah was to set up guerrilla networks in many of the refugee camps. Historian Helena Cobban describes their activities: "The guerrilla commanders . . . tried to prepare the local population to [fight against Israel] both through organizing passive resistance to Israeli military rule and by giving rudimentary military training to recruits."[22] During the late 1960s, for instance, the guerrillas, or fedayeen, issued instructions to civilians on how to make bombs and commit acts of sabotage. They also taught the population to spy on the enemy and to create Palestinian militant cells in every village.

The fedayeen of al-Fatah attacked Israeli targets by conducting raids across the border. Small groups of Palestinians bombed Israeli military equipment, and other fedayeen attacked Israeli soldiers and civilians. Raids and bombings of markets, movie houses, and apartment buildings occurred with great frequency, resulting in hundreds of Israeli deaths. Al-Fatah groups emerged in many countries, and by 1970 the organization had recruited and trained more than fifty thousand guerrillas.

The Six-Day War of 1967

Hoping to take advantage of the rising trend of nationalism and resistance among the Pal-estinians, the Arab nations of Egypt, Jordan, and Syria began to plot an invasion of Israel for the purpose of expanding their own borders and destroying the Israeli state. After learning of these plans, however, the Israeli army struck first and quickly gained impressive military victories over its Arab enemies.

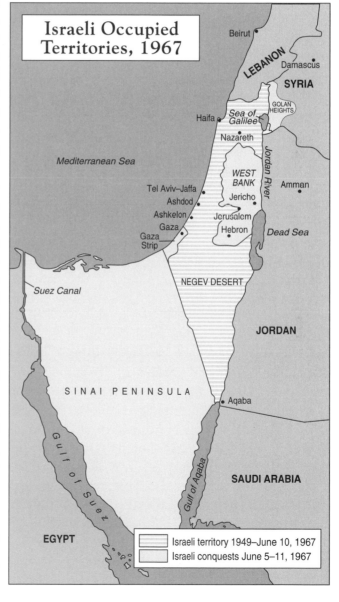

Israeli Occupied Territories, 1967

Israeli territory 1949–June 10, 1967
Israeli conquests June 5–11, 1967

In just six days, Israel won control of a vast amount of territory formerly controlled by the Arabs. These lands included the Gaza Strip, a coastal area along the eastern Mediterranean Sea; and the West Bank, an area formerly belonging to Jordan. Both of these regions were inhabited by hundreds of thousands of Palestinians living in refugee camps and in small villages and communities. In addition to the West Bank and the Gaza Strip, Israel also conquered the Sinai Peninsula, a huge area formerly belonging to Egypt; the Golan Heights, a Syrian territory; and East Jerusalem, a Jordanian enclave. These areas would henceforth be referred to as the occupied territories. The war also produced another 1 million Palestinian refugees who fled from Israeli armies. Many of these refugees joined their countrymen in the refugee camps and villages in the occupied territories.

After a cease-fire agreement was signed on June 5, 1967, the Israeli government began to send Israeli settlers into the newly acquired lands. It reasoned that Israel had won the land fairly during the warfare and thus Israelis had the right to live on it. This settlement, however, defied international law, which forbade a country from settling in an area that had been taken by military means. Indeed, within a few months of the war's end, the UN Security Council passed Resolution 242, calling on Israel to withdraw from these areas. The United Nations has continued to affirm this resolution every year since it was passed.

Yasir Arafat and the PLO

Although the Six-Day War had been devastating to the Arabs, it reinforced the resolve of Palestinians everywhere and strengthened their sense of nationalism. Al-Fatah and the fedayeen took advantage of the growing unrest among the Palestinians and increased their membership in the months following the war's end. Because of al-Fatah's growing prestige among Palestinians, Yasir Arafat was elected the chairman of the Palestine Liberation Organization in 1967. With Arafat's election, the PLO became the dominant force in the movement for Palestinian independence.

The new PLO charter that Arafat helped create was explicit in how this independence was to be won. It stated: "Only through battle, the spilling of blood, only with fire, death, and physical destruction, could total victory [against Israel] be won."[23] In twenty-nine of its thirty-three articles, the PLO National Covenant called for the destruction of Israel and, at one point, referred to Israel as an unmitigated evil.

Under Arafat, the PLO became known as the world's most violent guerrilla organization. Through the use of violence, Arafat and the PLO hoped to bring the plight of the Palestinian people to the world's attention. "As long as the world saw the Palestinians as no more than refugees standing in line for U.N. rations, it was not likely to respect them," Arafat once explained. "Now that the Palestinians carry rifles, the situation has changed."[24] Arafat and other Palestinian leaders also expressed their

Yasir Arafat

Yasir Ararat was born in Jerusalem on August 27, 1929. Arafat's given name is Abd al-Rahman Abd al-Rauf Arafat al-Qudwa al-Husseini, but he was nicknamed Yasir when he was a youth. At the age of twenty-two, Arafat obtained a degree in civil engineering at what is now the University of Cairo, Egypt. While there, he formed the General Union of Palestinian Students, a group that recruited students to fight for Palestinian independence.

During the late 1950s Arafat worked in Kuwait, where he formed a construction company and hired Palestinians to work for him. He founded the Movement for the Liberation of Palestine in 1961, a group that soon united with around thirty other Palestinian groups to form the nucleus of the militant group known as al-Fatah.

In 1967 Arafat was elected chairman of the Palestine Liberation Organization (PLO), a position he continues to hold. As leader of the PLO, Arafat has advocated and sponsored hundreds of terrorist attacks. Consolidating his power during the 1960s, 1970s, and 1980s, Arafat emerged as the undisputed leader of the Palestinian people, and he continues to dominate Palestinian politics today.

anger at the United States and Europe for their continued support of Israel. Hoping to strike back at these nations and Israel, the PLO turned to terrorism.

Acts of Terrorism

Palestinian terrorists carried out hundreds of attacks during the 1960s, 1970s, and 1980s. Numerous bombings and guerrilla attacks were conducted against thousands of Israeli citizens, settlers, and soldiers. The most dramatic terrorist tactic was the hijacking of airplanes. One of the most famous of these hijackings occurred in 1976 when Palestinian terrorists took 250 people hostage on a plane going from Israel to France. After landing in Entebbe, Uganda, the hijackers released all of the French passengers but took more than 100 Israeli passengers hostage. The terrorists demanded the

release of 53 convicted Palestinian terrorists held in Israeli prisons and set a forty-eight-hour deadline. If their demands were not met, the terrorists said, they would execute the Israeli passengers. Late at night on July 3, Israeli forces landed at Entebbe and, in a lightning attack, raided the airport and freed the hostages. One commando and 3 hostages were killed, along with all of the Palestinian terrorists.

Hundreds of other hijackings were also carried out, resulting in dozens of deaths of both passengers and terrorists. To successfully hijack planes, the Palestinians maintained a large network of airline employees from around the world to help them. Historian Julian Becker elaborates: "Among the employees of every airline, including those of Europe and the United States, there were hostesses and stewards bribed with monthly payments by the PLO."[25] These individuals were able to get special baggage on board, including arms and explosives, which could then be utilized by the terrorists to take control of the airliners.

The PLO also ran dozens of terrorist camps throughout the Middle East. Terrorists from West Germany, Italy, Northern Ireland, the United States, and many other nations visited and trained at these camps. The PLO used these trainees to carry out many terrorist attacks throughout the world. Hundreds of innocent civilians were killed in bombings of theaters, cafés, train stations, and department stores. These acts provoked international outrage and damaged support for the Palestinian cause.

Because terrorism had not helped gain international respect and assistance in the fight for Palestinian independence, Yasir Arafat changed tactics and appeared before the United Nations on November 13, 1974. In his speech to the members, Arafat portrayed the Palestinian people as victims of Israel and called on the international community to support Palestinian nationalism. In a dramatic and surprising statement, Arafat also denounced the use of terrorism. Many world leaders and political analysts questioned how sincere Arafat's denunciation of terror actually was, however. His statement had, in fact, come shortly after PLO representatives met with various other Palestinian groups to reaffirm their dedication to destroying Israel. One clause of a document they ap-

proved read, "The PLO will struggle by every means, the foremost of which is armed struggle, to liberate Palestinian land."[26] Other clauses approved the use of terrorist tactics to achieve the PLO's goals.

Despite his comments to the contrary, Arafat continued to advocate the use of terror and violence as a means of securing an independent Palestine. Using southern Lebanon as the primary base for PLO operations, Arafat ordered the fedayeen to continue their attacks on Israeli targets along the borders of Lebanon. The Palestinian guerrillas launched hundreds of attacks into Israel, hitting small targets and killing Israeli soldiers and civilians. Israel responded with air strikes and bombings that destroyed many refugee camps. Many Lebanese villages were also destroyed, leading the Lebanese government to ask the PLO to withdraw from the country. Arafat ignored the request and ordered the fedayeen to continue their incursions into Israel.

Retaliation

Israeli retaliations on refugee camps further galvanized the Palestinian community in its quest for independence and strengthened its hatred for Israel. Palestinian guerrillas responded with an increased level of violence all along the Lebanese border. Faced with continued defiance, the Israeli Defense Force launched a major military operation against the PLO in Lebanon in an effort to crush the fedayeen and al-Fatah. Death tolls ran very high. In one attack, Israeli bombs killed over two hundred

The Munich Olympics Massacre

Palestinian militants carried out hundreds of terrorist attacks during the 1960s and 1970s. One of the most infamous occurred during the 1972 Olympics held in Munich, Germany. Eight armed terrorists from the Palestinian group Black September, an extremist faction of the PLO, made a violent assault on a team of Israeli athletes gathered to participate in the games. Members of Black September said they were angry that Palestinian athletes were not allowed to participate in the Olympics. (When the Palestinian athletes petitioned for inclusion at the games, the Olympic Committee refused their request, asserting that Palestine was not a country.) The terrorists stated that they wanted to prove to the world that the Palestinians were a people with nationalist goals.

The Palestinian guerrillas held the eleven Israeli athletes for ransom in a dormitory. Because Israel refused to negotiate with the terrorists, the West German police decided to use force to secure the release of the athletes. Their rescue attempt failed, however, resulting in the deaths of the Israeli athletes and the Palestinian militants. Rather than earning world sympathy, as they had hoped, the terrorists caused international outrage and earned worldwide condemnation of Palestinian terrorism.

The Olympic flag flies at half-mast during the memorial service held for the Israeli athletes who were slain by Palestinian terrorists during the 1972 games in Munich.

Palestinian women and children who were hiding in the basement of a school. Lebanese hospitals were filled with the injured and wounded, over 75 percent of whom were Palestinian civilians.

The worst incident of violence during this period occurred on September 16, 1982, when the Kataeb, a Lebanese group supported by the Israeli army, attacked two Palestinian refugee camps known as Sabra and Shatila. The attack was in retaliation for the assassination of the Lebanese president, which was erroneously blamed on Palestinian forces. Although they did not participate in the violence, Israeli soldiers were given strict orders not to intervene with the Kataeb attack on the camps. According to eyewitnesses, the Israelis also blocked the exits, preventing Palestinians from escaping. A Palestinian who survived the attack later described what he had witnessed: "The killing was slow and methodical. . . . [The Kataeb's] assignment was carried out with rifles, knives, clubs, and chains. Groups of ten to twenty Palestinians were lined up

Speaking before the United Nations in 1974, Yasir Arafat declared that the world would decide whether the Palestinians would be its partners in peace or its enemies in war.

At camps known as Sabra and Shatila, Palestinian refugees were gunned down by Lebanese militants who mistakenly blamed them for the assassination of Lebanon's president.

against walls and machine-gunned. Mothers died clutching their babies. . . . Entire families spanning three generations perished."[27] Hundreds of Palestinian civilians lost their lives and hundreds more had their homes bulldozed to the ground.

World leaders and the international press later learned that the Palestinians at Sabra and Shatila were completely defenseless, despite Israeli accusations

that they were heavily armed. No evidence was ever found of either terrorists or weapons in the two camps. When the United Nations and the International Red Cross tried to investigate the killings, they were initially barred from entering the camps by Israeli troops. The same troops also blocked international relief efforts and prevented food and medical supplies from reaching the victims. World leaders strongly criticized

Medical crews carry victims of the massacre at Shatila. Israeli soldiers guarding the refugee camp apparently failed to intervene as the killings were taking place.

Israel for its failure to protect the Palestinian civilians and expressed sympathy for the Palestinian people.

The war in Lebanon, the massacre at Sabra and Shatila, and the struggles faced by the Palestinians in the 1960s, 1970s, and 1980s all fed the growing sense of nationalism within the Palestinian popula-tion. The hopes for Palestinian indepen-dence were universal throughout the camps and elsewhere. Samia, a forty-five-year-old East Jerusalem school supervi-sor, expressed this sense of solidarity when she stated, "We are one people. We are all Palestinians struggling together for in-dependence."[28]

CHAPTER 3

The Palestinian Authority

After decades of violence, Yasir Arafat announced in 1988 that he and the Palestine Liberation Organization were considering a more diplomatic approach to achieve independence and peace. By this point, the Israeli government was also ready to embrace diplomacy as a way to end the conflict. These shifting outlooks opened the door to the first-ever negotiations between the Palestinians and the Israelis. Historian David Lamb explains the climate that favored peace: "Despite spasms of violence, the war weariness of the Israelis and the Palestinians started nudging both sides towards peace."[29] The ensuing peace talks spurred the creation of a new organization that Palestinians hoped would lead them toward independence: the Palestinian Authority (PA).

The Creation of the Palestinian Authority

The Palestinian Authority was meant to govern Palestinian territory until a permanent Palestinian state could be formed. The PA would also take control of many social services, such as health care, education, and taxation. Its creation seemed to be a positive sign that the long years of struggle might be coming to an end because it was hoped that this new organization would be the first step toward Palestinian independence.

The formation of the Palestinian Authority was part of a complex peace agreement called the Oslo Accords. The Oslo Accords said that the Palestinians would recognize the right of Israel to exist and would denounce terrorism. For its part, Israel agreed to the creation of the Palestinian Authority

President Clinton presides over the historic handshake between Israeli prime minister Yitzhak Rabin and PLO chairman Yasir Arafat.

and to work toward an eventual Palestinian state. After negotiations were settled, Palestinian and Israeli leaders met in Washington, D.C., to sign the final agreement. History was made on September 13, 1992, when Palestinian leader Yasir Arafat held out his hand to Israeli prime minister Yitzhak Rabin while posing in front of the White House after signing the peace treaty.

The Oslo Accords detailed a five-year plan during which the Israelis would gradually withdraw from the West Bank and the Gaza Strip. The first withdrawal was to take place on December 13, 1993. The accords also decreed that the Israelis would slowly yield control over various aspects of government to the Palestinian Authority. At the end of the five-year period, there would be a permanent settlement based on UN resolutions that called for the complete withdrawal of Israeli forces from the occupied territories, resulting in the creation of a Palestinian state.

The Palestinian Authority Is Criticized

Shortly after the Oslo Accords were signed, Arafat was elected president of the Palestinian Authority, winning an overwhelming 85 percent of the vote. Arafat's critics, however, charged that the elections had been rigged in his favor. Arafat also came under attack from several Palestinian militant groups for having signed the Oslo Accords at all. These groups claimed that Arafat, in recognizing the right of Israel to exist, had betrayed the Palestinian cause, which had always been dedicated to the destruction of Israel. Also, by denouncing terrorism, they claimed, Arafat had abandoned his lifelong pledge to obtain Palestinian independence through violence. The militant groups believed that Palestinian freedom was not obtainable through negotiation, and so they continued to commit terrorist acts against Israel.

Within a few months after the formation of the PA, world leaders and political analysts also became critical of Arafat's leadership. For thirty years, Arafat had been the world's most recognizable terrorist; few believed the Palestinian leader would change his ways. As president of the Palestinian Authority, Arafat had promised reform and an end to violence, but in the eyes of world opinion, Arafat quickly reneged on both pledges. U.S. secretary of state Madeleine Albright spoke for many when she said, "It was soon evident that Arafat wasn't very good at his job."[30]

Palestinians grew critical of Arafat because he failed to effect any real change in the Palestinian-Israeli conflict. He could neither secure the release of Palestinian prisoners nor prevent nearly 150,000 Israeli settlers from moving into the occupied territories. And the Palestinian Authority could do little

The Palestinian Authority and Terrorism

As part of the Oslo Accords, the Palestinian Authority was charged with curbing terrorism, and during the mid-1990s it made several efforts to do so. Palestinian security forces routinely worked with Israeli troops and intelligence services to arrest terrorist suspects. Hundreds of Palestinian militants and terrorists were jailed as a result. However, terrorist attacks continued to occur, leading critics of the Palestinian Authority to charge that its efforts were not effective.

In addition to not preventing terrorism, it is widely suspected that Arafat and the PA have a hand in sponsoring such acts. For example, in January 2002 a boatload of weapons destined for the Palestinian Authority was intercepted by Israel, raising suspicions that PA support for terrorism continues. The Israelis also accuse Arafat of releasing suspected terrorists from prison, praising terrorist activity, and not cooperating with Israeli and international forces trying to curb terrorism. Some world leaders contend that Arafat and his al-Fatah faction even order terrorist attacks themselves. For these reasons, both Israel and the United States have increasingly refused to negotiate with Arafat until it can be confirmed that he has truly abandoned terrorism.

After signing a peace treaty with Israel, Yasir Arafat was condemned by Arab militants as a traitor. Many Palestinians continued to fight against Israel, thus undermining Arafat's authority.

about Israeli control of the movement of goods and people within the West Bank and the Gaza Strip. By May 1999, when the transition period was supposed to have been completed and the final issues addressed, the Israeli occupation of the West Bank and Gaza was still in full force. This reality caused many Palestinians to complain that they were no better off than before, and many blamed Ararat for the PA's failure.

The Responsibilities of the Palestinian Authority

Although it absorbed heavy criticism from all sides, the PA was still the only representative body of the Palestinians and was responsible for governing the land under its control. This was in itself a difficult task. The 1993 peace agreement had divided most of the West Bank and Gaza into individual areas, only some of which were under Palestinian control. Palestinian-held land was, for the most part, fragmented and isolated from other Palestinian areas—the areas were spread out far from each other, with Israeli-controlled territory in between. This made it difficult for the PA to adequately govern its territory because there was no contiguous landmass that could be called Palestine. In addition, Israel maintained security and military control of large areas of both the West Bank and the Gaza Strip, further impeding the PA from consolidating its control of Palestinian territory.

The Palestinian Authority is also responsible for providing such varied government services as education, criminal justice, health care, and trash collection for the Palestinians. Only in the area of health care was the PA able to show any degree of real success. The Palestinian Red Crescent Society, a Palestinian medical organization created in the late 1960s, expanded its responsibilities under the PA and was able to improve medical care in the occupied territories. The society built and maintained several modern hospitals in the Gaza Strip and the West Bank and provided medical personnel to meet a variety of Palestinian needs. The Red Crescent Society continues to provide much-needed physical and mental health care to Palestinian victims of trauma and violence.

In other areas of Palestinian life, however, the Palestinian Authority has been less successful. The primary reason for this lack of success has been a shortage of funds. Financial difficulties make it hard for the PA to provide basic public services, such as road improvements, trash pickup, fire protection, and crime prevention. The PA also struggles to pay the salaries of those employed by the government. These factors, along with the continued Israeli military presence, have made it difficult for the PA to improve the lives of Palestinians.

The Right of Return

Another important responsibility of the Palestinian Authority is to champion the issues that are important to the Palestinian people. The refugee issue is one such concern. The PA believes that Palestinians have the right to return to their former homes that are now in Israel, and it calls this a necessary step toward Palestinian independence. Palestinian leaders base their argument on a UN resolution that states, "The refugees wishing to return to their homes and live at peace with their neighbors should be permitted to do so at the earliest practical date, and . . . compensation should be paid for the property of those choosing not to return and for loss or damage to property."[31] The Arabic word for this issue is *Haq al-'Awda*, a word that means "justice."

If the millions of Palestinian refugees scattered all over the world were to return to their homeland in Israel, however, they would outnumber the Israelis. A majority Palestinian population would ultimately alter Israel's character, in effect destroying the Jewish state. Because of this, the PA recognizes that an actual return of refugees is unacceptable to Israel. The PA has indicated

U.S. Support for Israel

The Palestinian people are continually frustrated by America's unwavering support of Israel. The United States sends massive amounts of financial and military aid to Israel every year. The Palestinian Authority says this aid allows the Israelis to continue their domination over the Palestinian people.

Palestinians also argue that the United States allows Israel to frequently violate international law and ignore various UN resolutions. Historian David Lamb recorded the feelings of a Palestinian guerrilla in his book *The Arabs*: "I'll tell you what this war has taught us. It taught us that the real enemy is the United States. It is against you that we must fight. Not just because your bombs killed our people, but because you have closed your eyes to what is moral and just." Many Palestinians today share this opinion.

its willingness to compromise on that issue in exchange for the Israelis recognizing their responsibility in creating the refugee problem in 1948. It asks that Israel acknowledge the Palestinians' political and moral right to return.

The Israelis are unwilling to do this. Israel fears that acknowledgment might lead to new Palestinian demands for the return of refugees. However, Israel did agree during the 2000 peace talks to allow ten thousand refugees to return to their families. Israeli negotiators remained steadfast in their refusal to accept any culpability in the creation of the refugee situation. Historian David K. Shipler offers his impressions of the Israeli position: "Israel is not ready to accept the fact that some of its finest heroes expelled Arabs, for to do so would be an acknowledgment . . . of some legitimate Arab claim to property or compensation."[32] With the Palestinians and the Israelis unable to arrive at a compromise, the issue of the right of return remains unresolved.

The Issue of Jerusalem

The Palestinian Authority is also adamant about Palestinians' right to Jerusalem. The issue of Jerusalem is very sensitive, as both the Israelis and the Palestinians claim the city as their capital, and each revere the city as holy. For Jews, it is the site of the First Temple and the Wailing Wall; for Muslims, it is where Muhammad ascended to heaven from the Dome of the Rock. For Christians, it is the city where Jesus lived and died; it is also the site of the Holy Sepulcher, where Jesus was buried and is said to have returned from the dead. Most of the holy sites for all three religions are centered in the Old City, which is located in East Jerusalem, a predominantly Palestinian area.

The conflict over the control of Jerusalem is a long and complex one. The United Nations attempted to settle the issue in 1948 when, in addition to recommending the partition of the entire region, it proclaimed that the city of Jerusalem should come under international control. This would have

Because Muslims consider the Dome of the Rock (pictured) and other sites to be sacred, Jewish control of Jerusalem is a sore point in Arab-Israeli negotiations.

guaranteed that Jerusalem remain neutral, a part of neither the state of Israel nor an anticipated Palestinian state. During the war in 1948–1949, however, Israeli forces won control over West Jerusalem. Meanwhile, the Jordanians captured the eastern half of the city. In the Six-Day War in 1967, Israel captured the eastern half of the city from Jordan, resulting in complete Israeli control over the city. The area, along with its hundreds of thousands of Palestinian residents, has remained under Israeli governance since that time.

In various peace negotiations of the late twentieth century, Palestinian leaders demanded that a Palestinian state must have East Jerusalem as its capital. The PA stresses that Jerusalem has for centuries been an important Islamic center and an essential part of the larger Islamic world. The city's religious significance, it says, along with its access to international markets, make it critical to an independent Palestinian state. The Israelis, however, hold similar religious and political claims to the city, making this an issue that continually hinders peace negotiations.

The Israeli Settlements

Another issue on the PA's agenda is the presence of Israeli settlements in the West Bank and Gaza. The movement of Israeli settlers into Palestinian territory began in earnest following the Six-Day War, when Israel took over the West Bank and the Gaza Strip. The Israeli government encouraged its citizens to move to the newly acquired land, arguing it had been won fairly in war and thus was reasonable for Israelis to take advantage of it. During the ensuing years, hundreds of thousands of Israelis moved into these areas. Israel's expansion of the settlements was aggressive, with the population of settlers nearly doubling between the years 1992 and 2000. As of 2000, there were 130 settlements in the West Bank and 16 in Gaza.

The PA argues that the settlements are illegal because they are built on Palestinian territory. Moreover, it stresses that Palestinian land is so fragmented by the Israeli settlements that governing the West Bank and the Gaza Strip is nearly impossible. Each settlement is also guarded by the Israeli military, whose activities disrupt the lives of Palestinian residents in nearby villages. For example, the settlements submit the Palestinians to numerous roadblocks, preventing the movement of people and goods from area to area.

The city of Nablus, for instance, includes eight Palestinian villages, two refugee camps, and has a population of nearly two hundred thousand inhabitants. It is surrounded by eight Israeli settlements with a population of six thousand. Despite the disparity in population, control of this city is entirely in Israeli hands. Nablus and other Israeli settlements, the PA asserts, are like armed fortresses, guarded by soldiers and armed civilians. At many Israeli settlements, Jewish settlers patrol the streets with submachine guns slung over their shoulders, acting as self-appointed security forces. Palestinians are not allowed to travel on many roads that con-

Israeli Settlements in the West Bank and Gaza Strip

Jordan River

Jenin

WEST BANK

Nablus

Qalqilya

Mediterranean Sea

ISRAEL

Ramallah

Jericho

Jerusalem

Bethlehem

Gaza

GAZA STRIP

Hebron

Dead Sea

JORDAN

△ Israeli Settlements

nect Jewish settlements. In some cases this leaves entire Palestinian villages isolated and cut off from one another.

The PA also points out the enormous disparity between the Israeli settlers and the Palestinians who live nearby. This disparity is one reason for the PA's call for removal of all Israeli settlements.

Most of the Israeli settlements are similar to American suburbs, complete with brick homes, swimming pools, recreation centers, and modern schools. They are completely self-sufficient, with grocery stores, profitable businesses, large farms, and government facilities. The Palestinians, on the other hand, either live in villages with simple homes or in refugee camps in crowded shacks and cement-block housing without access to water or electricity. The refugees' lifestyle, for the most part, is one of poverty, deprivation, and isolation, while those who live in villages and small towns must struggle to make ends meet. Former U.S. secretary of state Madeleine Albright described this incongruency after a visit to the area in the late 1990s: "Within gated settlement walls were [Israeli] people with money living well. Outside were shacks and Palestinians living impoverished lives."[33]

Mahmoud, an unemployed electrical engineer, describes the settlements and his life in the West Bank: "We're living in one huge prison. . . . The settlements are expanding and expanding. There is no space [for the Palestinians]. Here you find fifty Palestinians living in one house, and the Israelis have all the open areas."[34] This situation is decried by the Palestinians. Yasir Arafat and the Palestinian Authority have repeatedly asserted that there can be no equitable peace until the Israeli settlements have been dismantled.

The Future of the Palestinian Authority

The Palestinian Authority's ability to negotiate a peace settlement has been severely hampered in recent years by financial concerns. The organization is, in fact, on the verge of bankruptcy with a $300 million deficit. Many economic analysts predict that, by the end of 2004, the PA will be unable to pay the salaries of its own workers. Because of

Palestinian Complaints About Media Bias

The Palestinians claim that the Western media consistently report news from the Middle East in a pro-Israeli manner. They complain their voices are not heard and their viewpoints are absent from news broadcasts, especially those in the United States. It is also thought that the Western media tend to focus solely on the terrorist tactics of the Palestinians and ignore other aspects of their society.

The Palestinian Authority also argues that Western media sources downplay the damage that Israel inflicts on Palestinians. Shaaban, a Palestinian who lives in the West Bank, voiced his disappointment to author Wendy Pearlman in her book *Occupied Voices: Stories of Everyday Life from the Second Intifada:* "When something happens to the Israelis, the whole world is enraged. Meanwhile we die by the hundreds and no one does a thing, as if they don't even know about it."

A Palestinian family lives under a tent in Jenin after their home was destroyed in a security sweep by Israeli soldiers.

the failure of the PA to enact reforms and curb terrorism, the United States and many European nations have withheld promised loans and funds, leaving the PA with even less money.

This situation is further compounded by allegations that Arafat has embezzled vast sums of money from PA accounts. In 2004 French authorities began investigating Arafat's wife (who lives in Paris) for money laundering, and they discovered that over $10 million had been transferred to Mrs. Arafat's bank account from a Swiss bank. Many political and financial an-

alysts believe that much of this money came from foreign contributions to the PA. During the last decade, the Palestinian Authority has received over $5 billion in foreign aid, mostly from the European Union. An independent audit recently discovered that close to $1 billion of that money could not be accounted for. Auditors suspect much of this amount ended up in Mrs. Arafat's account.

The Palestinian Authority has also been charged with corruption and violating the civil rights of Palestinians. Numerous reports of embezzling, bribery,

French authorities are investigating allegations that Yasir Arafat's wife, Suha Arafat, helped her husband embezzle money from the Palestine Authority into Paris bank accounts.

and murder have been made public in recent years. One of the most serious charges is that the PA has murdered Palestinians who protest against the government. Journalist Erika Waak writes, "For over a decade, the PA has violated Palestinians' human rights and civil liberties by routinely killing civilians—including collaborators, demonstrators, journalists, and others—without charge or fair trial."[35] Thousands of Palestinians have lost their lives, not at the hands of the Israelis, but at the hands of their own representatives.

As a result of failing finances and corruption within the organization, the PA is on the verge of collapse. Journalists John Ward Anderson and Molly Moore of the *Washington Post* report on the severity of the situation: "The Palestinian Authority is broke, politically fractured, riddled with corruption, unable to provide security for its own people, and seemingly unwilling to crack down on terrorist attacks against Israel."[36] The possible collapse of the PA would leave a serious political vacuum in the West Bank and Gaza and put an effective end to Palestinian negotiating efforts. If this happens, the hopes for an independent Palestinian state will face even further difficulties.

CHAPTER 4

Perpetrators and Victims

Violence in the Holy Land has become a daily occurrence. Sadly, Israelis and Palestinians are both perpetrators and victims of this violence. Palestinian terrorist attacks occur with increasing regularity and lead to Israeli reprisals with air strikes and military incursions. Hardly a day goes by in the region without the reports of deaths and injuries on both sides, greatly hampering all efforts at peace.

The First Intifada

Violence drastically increased toward the end of the 1980s, when, frustrated by the long years under Israeli occupation, a peaceful Palestinian demonstration in the Gaza Strip erupted into a riot that soon spread throughout the occupied territories. Palestinians picked up the only weapons they had available— stones and rocks—and threw them at the Israeli forces, who fought from tanks and helicopters. These actions were completely independent of Yasir Arafat and the Palestine Liberation Organization; they were the result of ordinary Palestinians expressing outrage at their situation. The uprising became known as the intifada, which in Arabic means "to shake off."

The intifada was embraced by nearly all Palestinians. Schoolchildren, donning ski masks, threw stones at the soldiers and tanks the Israeli government sent in to subdue the riots. Palestinian adults used homemade bombs and rocks as weapons and set numerous fires throughout the region. Israeli troops responded by firing tear gas into the demonstrators and by shooting many of the attackers when they felt personally threatened. Many Israeli groups, along with U.S. officials, condemned the violence and defended Israel's response. Former secretary of state Madeleine Albright, for instance, stated, "Palestinian rock throwers placed Israel under siege and . . . Israeli occupation forces were simply defending themselves."[37]

Seeing young children shot on television by heavily armed Israeli soldiers, however, shocked most of the world. Israel was strongly criticized by many world leaders for its use of guns, tanks, and helicopters to combat the lightly armed resisters. Historian Karen Armstrong elaborates: "All around the world, the general public became aware of the aggressive nature of the Israeli oc-

cupation . . . when they saw armed Israeli soldiers chasing and gunning down stone-throwing children."[38]

Hamas and Suicide Bombers

The violence that erupted among the Palestinian population sparked the rise of a new Palestinian terrorist group called Hamas. Dedicated to the destruction of Israel through violent means, Hamas appealed to Palestinians who felt terrorism was their only weapon against the Israelis. Hamas recruited thousands of Palestinian men, women, and children to give up their lives in order to serve the cause of Palestinian independence. Palestinian Fadal

Security in Israel

Because of deadly suicide bombings, security in Israel has become extremely tight. Security at stores, malls, movie theaters, and other recreational places usually features airport-style checks and searches. To get into a shopping mall, for example, one must wait in line just to get into the parking lot. An armed security guard usually looks into the face of every person in each car and inspects the trunk. In some malls, additional guards scan the parking lot from watchtowers. At the entrance to the mall, bags and purses are scanned, and shoppers must lift their arms to be checked by a metal-detecting wand. Inside the mall, other armed guards are visible, and some major stores have their own security to make one final check of anyone entering.

This is life in Israel today. Although deadly bombings are nothing new, in recent times watchfulness has greatly increased as a result of a number of suicide bombings inside public places. Such measures have met with some amount of success, as Israeli authorities have been able to stop some bombers before they strike. Still, such efforts do not stop bombings entirely. In one event, a bomber who realized that she would not get past security at a market in Jerusalem simply walked to a nearby bus stop and blew herself up there. In another incident, bombers did not even try to board a bus but instead pulled up alongside it and, in a massive detonation, blew up their car and the bus. Such suicide bombings have terrorized Israelis and have made them increasingly unwilling to negotiate with Palestinians until the terrorists are reeled in.

Hamodah explained the willingness of his people to volunteer: "We are ready to sacrifice our bodies to liberate our land and Jerusalem. . . . [The members of Hamas] are not terrorists, they are sacrificing themselves for our land."[39]

Hamas's primary method of operation is suicide bombing. This is a particularly effective form of terrorism that generates intense fear among those who are targeted because it is never known when or where a suicide bomber will strike. In most cases, explosives are strapped to the suicide bomber's body and are then detonated in a crowded location. The bomber is killed, along with other people. On January 29, 2004, for instance, a suicide bomber detonated a fifteen-pound bag of explosives on board a crowded Israeli bus, killing at least ten and wounding fifty bystanders.

Hamas has taken responsibility for most of the suicide bombings that have occurred in Israel since the 1990s.

Israeli investigators inspect the wreckage of a bus blown apart by a suicide bomber. The militant group Hamas claimed responsibility for this deadly attack.

These have become frequent and deadly. Between 2001 and April 2004, 377 Israelis were killed in 425 Hamas suicide bombings, Israeli sources say. Hamas claims that the suicide attacks are in retaliation for continued Israeli occupation of the West Bank and the Gaza Strip and regards them as a legitimate and effective way of liberating the Palestinians.

The Israeli government and most world leaders decisively condemn suicide bombings. Many Palestinians, however, view suicide bombers as heroes; they deeply respect the fact that they give their lives for the Palestinian cause. Indeed, after a suicide bomber strikes, the streets of the West Bank and the Gaza Strip are lined with glossy posters honoring the person as a martyr who will go straight to heaven. David Lamb explains this kind of thinking: "Fanatics in the Middle East regard terrorists as . . . young and glamorous and nationalistic and daring. They face death stoically . . . and in death they earn recognition and are exalted."[40]

Although suicide bombers are typically men, women have increasingly joined the ranks of those willing to kill and be killed in the struggle for Palestinian independence. One such woman is Reem al-Reyashi, a twenty-two-year-old Palestinian woman who, on January 13, 2004, left her two young children at home, strapped on a bomb, and then blew herself up, killing four Israelis in the process. In a taped message she made prior to the bombing, al-Reyashi said, "I have always wanted . . . to carry out a martyrdom operation."[41] She joined several other Palestinian women who had carried out such attacks. Perhaps the best known of these women is Wafa Idriss, a Palestinian nurse who, on January 27, 2002, walked into a Jerusalem shopping area and detonated a bomb that killed 1 person and injured 150 others.

Glorifying Martyrs

Every death of a Hamas militant is used by the organization to glorify its cause. After a suicide bombing, a Hamas unit arrives at the morgue with a loudspeaker and plays the group's funeral song, a stirring tune that is readily recognizable to Palestinians. Another unit organizes volunteers to carry the body, which is draped in a green Hamas flag, while a third unit goes to the militant's home and prepares food and other refreshments for the mourners. Families of suicide bombers also receive financial compensation for their loss, which can be quite valuable to very poor families. The special attention Hamas showers on the families of fallen Palestinians has earned the organization a great deal of support in the West Bank and the Gaza Strip.

Thus far, the Israeli military and security forces have been unable to prevent the suicide attacks. The bombers attack at random, choosing their locations with no apparent pattern or logic, leaving it difficult if not impossible to predict where the next bombing will occur. Because of this unpredictability, many Israeli citizens live in constant fear that they will be the next victim. Jeffrey Klein, an Israeli resident, responded to one of the bus bombings in this way: "There was just another bomb, this time in Tel Aviv. . . . Again. And again. And again. Why can't they leave us alone? Why aren't we allowed to just live in our homeland in peace?"[42] The Israelis have responded to these threats by increasing security at border crossings and by attacking suspected terrorist hideouts, but these efforts have done little to decrease the number of Israeli deaths and injuries.

Further complicating efforts to eradicate suicide bombings is the fact that Hamas has been able to continually enlist new ranks of Palestinians to take the place of those who blow themselves up. When a suicide operative dies, Hamas has teams of dedicated recruiters working to replenish its army of terrorists. Recruiters flock to Palestinian mosques, schools, and community centers to talk to young people about Hamas's mission to free Palestine. Convinced that attacking Israel is the only way to end the armed occupation of their territory, hundreds of young people sign up for training. This steady influx of new members enables the Hamas organization to continue its attacks on Israeli targets.

Hamas members also are able to evade Israeli capture because of their ability to blend into Palestinian society. Hamas militants have little difficulty concealing themselves among ordinary Palestinians, who are sometimes willing to offer them shelter and protection. Indeed, Hamas members are frequently protected by Palestinian villagers and refugees who see terrorism as the only way to achieve independence.

Palestinian Violence During the Second Intifada

Suicide bombings have been the primary feature of what is called the second Palestinian intifada, which began in September 2000. Much of the violence has originated in the refugee camps in the occupied territories. The camps are strongholds of radical groups like Hamas, Islamic Jihad (a group working toward the destruction of Israel and the creation of an Islamic Palestine), and the al-Aqsa Martyrs' Brigade (a terrorist offshoot of al-Fatah). All three groups use suicide bombings as their primary weapon. Together the groups have been responsible for thousands of deaths and injuries since the start of the second intifada.

In addition to the organized efforts of terrorist groups, individual Palestinians in the camps and elsewhere have killed hundreds of Israeli soldiers as part of sustained resistance to the occupation. Palestinians have used a variety of weapons and methods to harass and harm the soldiers. Homemade bombs, land mines, and burning barricades block the entrance to many camps and villages, and Palestinian snipers armed with assault rifles target Israeli forces. In recent years, the Palestinians have also smuggled missile launchers into the region through underground tunnels that allow them free passage from the refugee camps to Egypt. As a consequence, when the Israeli army enters the camps, it is often met with bursts of gunfire and rocket attacks.

The coffin of Reem al-Reyashi, a female Hamas suicide bomber, is carried through the streets of Gaza in 2004.

Palestinian Victims of Violence

While some Palestinians are perpetrators and supporters of violence, many thousands of others are the victims of the powerful Israeli army. Every day they face possible injury or death when the Israeli military rolls into Palestinian towns, looking to round up suspected terrorists and their supporters. During the period between November 2000 and April 2002, for instance, an estimated fifteen hundred Palestinians were killed and over twenty thousand were injured as a result of the Israeli incursions. Unarmed Palestinian civilians have been injured or killed walking down the street, standing in their front yards, shopping at the market, crossing a checkpoint, or sitting in their homes with their families.

The Israeli government orders these incursions to respond to suicide attacks and other acts of violence, but the Palestinians charge that Israel's response

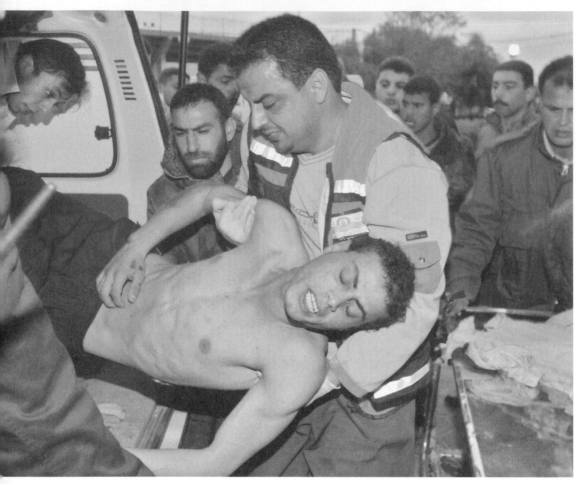

A wounded Palestinian youth is loaded into an ambulance after Israeli soldiers raided his refugee camp in retaliation for militants' attacks in Gaza.

is indiscriminate in its focus and scope. Instead of limiting the violence to a particular person or home, for example, the Israeli army will frequently destroy a whole block of homes, killing or injuring innocent people along with those suspected of wrongdoing. In this way, entire communities are punished for violence committed by just a few individuals.

The Palestinians also complain that Israel matches every Palestinian terrorist attack with a tougher and more violent counterblow. After a suicide bombing, the Israeli army frequently attacks suspected hotbeds of terrorism with helicopter attacks, airplane bombings, and tank deployments. Palestinians say this is an excessive response to the violence committed by Palestinian militants and gunmen. Such Israeli attacks often kill hundreds, many of whom are often innocent bystanders who have no connection to terrorist activities.

Palestinians also claim that whole families are arrested if a family member

Destruction of Palestinian Homes

Israeli occupying forces have destroyed hundreds of Palestinian homes since the second intifada began in September 2000. Palestinian leaders claim that many of the homes are destroyed to make room for more Israeli settlements or to take control of the most fertile areas of the occupied territories. The Palestinian Authority has repeatedly criticized the Israelis for violating an international law that prohibits the destruction of personal property in an occupied region.

The Israeli government defends its actions by saying that many Palestinians shelter terrorists in their homes, and that Israel has a right to protect itself from suicide bombers. Israeli leaders also contend that their military forces are searching for tunnels under Palestinian homes, which are used to smuggle arms and explosives into Palestinian areas and to move terrorists in and out of the occupied territories.

The destruction has devastated many Palestinian neighborhoods. Mounds of rubble fill many streets, and residents of West Bank and Gaza communities live in constant fear that their homes might be destroyed with them still inside. Entire Palestinian villages have been leveled, thousands of homes destroyed, and countless Palestinians made homeless since the beginning of the second intifada.

A Palestinian boy carries belongings from his wrecked home in one of the West Bank settlements.

has been accused of a crime, and they call this response unfair and excessive. In another example of excessive aggression, communities are frequently isolated and restricted in their movements while Israeli soldiers search for militants. Human Rights Watch, one of many groups monitoring the violence in the occupied territories, has confirmed that the Israeli military frequently utilizes "excessive and indiscriminate use of lethal force [and] arbitrary killings . . . that far exceed any possible military necessity."[43]

Palestinian leaders have taken this condemnation a step further, suggesting that such Israeli acts of violence are, in fact, terrorist attacks. Historian David Lamb elaborates on this charge: "Israeli air raids that kill innocents in Palestinian villages may be carried out in the name of self-defense, but to the recipients that is just a euphemism for terrorism. Why, . . . [the Palestinians] ask, is violence condoned as justified when undertaken by one group and condemned as uncivilized barbarity when committed by another?"[44]

Large numbers of Palestinians witness and are victims of Israeli attacks on a daily basis. As a result, many lead desperate and fearful lives. This reality has led to growing support for the more radical and militant elements of Palestinian society that advocate the destruction of Israel. Feeling helpless to stop the violence perpetrated against them, thousands of Palestinians have joined the ranks of Hamas and other terrorist organizations, believing that only by fighting back can they hope to effect any positive change in their lives.

Violence and Palestinian Children

Many Palestinian children witness and experience violence and death on a daily basis. It is estimated, in fact, that over half of all Palestinian children have witnessed beatings and killings, and nearly 40 percent have been the victims of violence themselves. Children report not being able to sleep because of the sound of gunfire throughout the night. Others fear leaving the house because they might be beaten or killed by Israeli soldiers or settlers. Not a week passes in the occupied territories, in fact, without the reported death of a child. Palestinian Alexandra Avakian reports on the effects of such violence: "The children of [the territories] are very damaged. . . . Their faces have traces of trouble, and worry, and fear."[45]

Seldom do Palestinian children play in the carefree way that children in more secure parts of the world play. When they play and when they go to school, they have to confront Israeli soldiers who patrol the streets outside their homes and schools. The constant fear of injury or death have led many children to turn to violence themselves. Palestinian Ammar Abu Zayyad said of his childhood: "There is a great difference between my childhood and that of other children in the world. I opened my eyes on a world that didn't give me any rights. So I put aside my toys and retrieved the stone [that is, turned to

Mourners pray during the funeral for two young Palestinian boys killed in clashes between Palestinians and Israeli troops.

violence]—the only thing that made me feel better."[46]

This exposure to violence has scarred Palestinian children; many suffer from emotional problems that include the inability to sleep, fear of the darkness and of strangers, fear of loud noises, and fear of leaving home. They also experience nightmares, bedwetting, hyperactivity, and increased aggressiveness. Most children report that they feel unsafe and believe that their parents are unable to protect them.

The Deaths of Palestinian Children

Children are repeatedly killed and injured in the occupied territories. Most of these wounds result from simply being in the wrong place at the wrong time. Many get caught in cross fire between Palestinians and Israeli troops; others are injured because of their proximity to protesters or their participation in rebellious acts, and still others because they threaten Israeli soldiers.

Palestinian children hurl rocks at Israeli tanks. Palestinian children are often killed or wounded during such incidents.

Most Israeli soldiers do not intend to kill or injure children. Confronted daily by protesters and students shouting obscenities and hurling stones, many of the soldiers live in fear for their own lives, knowing that a sniper's bullet can end their life at any time. As a result, soldiers often react quickly to threats and may shoot without identifying their target. An Israeli officer named Myron spoke to reporter Tad Szulc about how easy it is to make a mistake. "[You see] a guy aiming a gun. . . . What do you do? You shoot. [Then you find out that] the gun wasn't a gun, it was a broomstick painted black. You're still killing a child. . . . I hate it. In a war you can be idealistic and fight for a cause. But [in the territories] we're fighting children and women."[47]

Whether killed accidentally or on purpose, hundreds of Palestinian children have lost their lives. During the first three months of the second intifada, for example, more than one-third of all Palestinians killed by Israeli soldiers were children. One such child was an eleven-year-old boy named Khalil al-Mughrabi, who was shot from an Israeli guard tower while flying a kite. Caught in a cross fire between Palestinian demonstrators and Israeli soldiers, two other boys were shot and wounded when they tried to drag Khalil's body to safety. Such tragedies are common throughout the West Bank and the Gaza Strip.

The death of a seven-year-old first grader in the Aida refugee camp on November 11, 1997, drew particularly swift condemnation from Palestinian lead-ers. While not taking part in a Palestinian demonstration himself, the boy was watching a group of children throw stones at nearby soldiers. Gunfire suddenly erupted from both sides. Ahmed Salah, a mechanic, witnessed the violence that ensued and told reporters, "One of the [Israeli] soldiers grabbed a boy, threw him on the ground and placed his boot over the boy's neck. The soldier then leaned down on his other knee, aimed his sniper gun and fired at [his] head."[48] The boy was in a coma for five days before succumbing to his injuries. The Israelis assert that such deaths are provoked by the Palestinians and their continued violent demonstrations against the Israeli military.

Palestinian parents live with the constant knowledge that their children might be injured or killed. Muna, the mother of a fifteen-year-old boy who was killed by the Israelis, states, "We used to dream that our children would grow up."[49] Lamenting on the loss of land and country, Palestinian parents blame the Israelis for also taking their children from them.

Attacks on Medical Personnel

Palestinian leaders contend that Palestinian hospitals and medical personnel are often targets of the Israeli forces. The Red Crescent Society, the leading provider of Palestinian health care, documented nearly two hundred attacks on Palestinian hospitals, ambulances, and medical personnel between September 2000 and April 2002. The society reported that, on at least three occasions, doctors or ambulance drivers were killed while driving to work or while treating patients in the streets. The Israelis deny that the physicians or paramedics were themselves the targets; rather, they claim that the medical personnel were caught in either cross fire or were the victims of random shootings.

The Palestinians accuse the Israelis of deliberately attacking hospitals and disrupting patient care. On March 8, 2002, for instance, the Al-Yamama Hospital in Bethlehem came under fire when Israeli tanks raided the city. After several rounds of tank fire damaged the building, Israeli troops stormed the halls of the hospital in full riot gear, carrying machine guns and looking for Palestinian terrorists who frequently use such facilities as hiding places. The soldiers did a room-to-room search for militants before leaving the facility. Pa-

tients and staff alike complained of being forcibly held in community rooms while the search took place. While no deaths occurred in this attack, several patients and nurses were injured.

Palestinian leaders claim that this kind of violence is prohibited by international law, which considers medical facilities, doctors, nurses, and ambulances as neutral observers and not targets during wars or rebellions. According to the Palestinians and dozens of human rights organizations, Israel has repeatedly ignored this neutrality.

A Typical Day of Violence

Violence and death have become a way of life for Palestinians living in the West Bank and Gaza. February 8, 2004, was a typical day for the Palestinians, as *Time* correspondent Johanna McGeary reports:

Palestinian Prisoners

It is estimated that the Israelis have imprisoned some two hundred thousand Palestinians since the 1980s. The majority of prisoners have been arrested because of violent acts against Israel but others have been arrested for vague or minor offenses. Indeed, many Palestinians accuse the Israelis of fabricating and exaggerating charges against Palestinians. For example, in Wendy Pearlman's book *Occupied Voices: Stories of Everyday Life from the Second Intifada*, a Palestinian man named Sultan says: "I spent three years in jail. And do you know what my crime was? I was asked if I like Fatah [a terrorist group] and I said 'yeah, I like Fatah.' That's it. I didn't do anything more than that."

Palestinians also complain they are mistreated in Israeli jails. They say they often receive no water for long periods, are not allowed to go to the toilet, and are seldom given blankets to keep them warm. Many Palestinian prisoners have said they have been abused and tortured in Israeli jails and prisons, which many human rights groups confirm. Prisoners have reported long hours of interrogation, threats made against family members, beatings, and other forms of physical abuse they are forced to endure.

Two Palestinians killed; thirty-five wounded, including fourteen children; fourteen arrested; sixteen residential and eleven business buildings damaged; forty-four acres of land confiscated; sixteen houses demolished; seven cars damaged; two checkpoints installed; . . . and twenty-two incidents of bombing or heavy machine-gun fire from IDF [Israeli Defense Forces] troops.[50]

While these statistics vary from day to day, seldom do the Palestinians experience a reprieve from the violence. Israelis also endure constant attacks and bombings in their cities and towns.

When a Palestinian suicide bomber strikes a target in Israel, an otherwise ordinary day erupts into pandemonium for those Israelis in the vicinity. The sound of the explosion is heard for miles around, as windows shatter and pieces of glass, metal, and other materials crash through nearby structures and automobiles. Flying debris often injures hundreds of bystanders, while those occupying the targeted building or vehicle are killed instantly. The wails of ambulance, fire, and police sirens fill the air as rescue workers descend on the scene. The devastation of such attacks is compounded by the knowledge that the Palestinian terrorists will strike again. The fear comes from never knowing when, where, or who will suffer.

This kind of never-ending violence has a devastating impact on the lives of both Palestinians and Israelis. The constant threat of injury or death heightens the level of fear, mistrust, and hatred that the two groups feel for each other. There are few families who have not been personally affected by the violence in some form, whether it is the death of a family member, the injury of another, or the destruction of their property. The violence continues unabated with no apparent end in sight.

CHAPTER 5

Life in the West Bank and the Gaza Strip

Life in the West Bank and the Gaza Strip is a day-to-day struggle to survive. In addition to having to contend with daily violence, the Palestinians have also been ravaged by poverty, deteriorating health, school closures, food shortages, unemployment, and an increasing sense of hopelessness. They live under frequent curfews and restrictions, free speech is limited, and they cannot travel without proper documentation. Palestinians rarely get to see their families in other countries, or even in other parts of the West Bank and the Gaza Strip.

Many Palestinians have grown up in these conditions, and they have never known any other kind of life. Samia, an elementary school supervisor, speaks for many Palestinians when she says, "You don't know what occupation means unless you go through it. It puts an end to your freedom, even your freedom of thinking. . . . It is the loss of human dignity that is the worst part of occupation. We are treated like a herd of sheep."[51]

The Restriction of Movement

Since the beginning of the second intifada in 2000, Palestinians in the West Bank and Gaza have frequently been prevented from moving from town to town and between the territories and Israel. The Israeli army enforces curfews and road closures to allow troops to move freely in the occupied territories during searches for Palestinian militants. The closures have also been imposed in an attempt to curb Palestinian riots and attacks on Israeli soldiers. The restrictions and closures have impacted every aspect of the Palestinians' day-to-day life.

Entire Palestinian communities have been placed under curfews that confine them to their homes for days and weeks at a time. Under these curfews, the Palestinians are able to leave their homes only for a few hours every four or five days to buy groceries and obtain other necessities. Between June 21 and September 27, 2002, the town of Nablus, for instance, was under curfew a total of 2,292 hours out of 2,376 hours. Any Palestinian who ventures outside during these restrictions risks being arrested for disobeying Israeli military law.

The Israelis have placed stringent restrictions on Palestinian travel in the occupied territories. Hoping to prevent the movement of Palestinian terrorists into Israel, the Israeli army can restrict and stop all Palestinian traffic if it is searching for terrorists. Israeli defense minister Binyamin Ben Eliezer explained the army's orders in October 2002: "The directives of the military command are to freeze all traffic on West Bank roads, including taxis, buses, private vehicles, and others according to security needs."[52] Once stopped, Palestinian vehicles are searched for illegal arms and militants.

These security measures have taken a great toll on the Palestinian population. Traveling even a short distance usually takes a very long time. Concrete barriers, dirt piles, deep trenches, and manned Israeli checkpoints block the primary roads to many villages and cities, delaying Palestinian vehicles for hours at a time. To avoid these roadblocks,

An Israeli soldier watches Palestinians pass a security checkpoint in the West Bank. Such restrictions on travel disrupt the daily routine for most Palestinians.

An Israeli armored vehicle blocks traffic outside Ramallah. Many Palestinians risk arrest by driving on back roads in order to avoid these roadblocks.

many Palestinians travel miles out of their way on unpaved back roads. In recent years, however, Israeli soldiers have begun patrolling these roads as well with orders to stop any Palestinian vehicle and arrest the passengers. The curfews, closures, and travel restrictions have thus virtually imprisoned hundreds of thousands of Palestinians within their own communities.

Because of Gaza's reputation as a hotbed of radicalism and terrorism, the Israelis have been particularly stringent in their efforts to root out militants in that region. This has caused a great hardship for the nearly 1 million Palestinians who live in the Gaza Strip. Palestinian Alexandra Avakian explains: "Most Gazans can't get permission to go anywhere outside Gaza—anywhere. . . . There are people who, if they come back to visit their families and the border is shut . . . they can't go back. . . . So Gaza is very much like a prison camp."[53]

The Effect of Restrictions on the Economy

The various closures, curfews, and restrictions have also had a devastating impact on the Palestinian economy. Before the restrictions were enforced, Palestinian business owners were able to send their goods to international markets on ships leaving Palestinian port cities and aircraft leaving Gaza International Airport. With the port cities and the airport now closed, merchants are unable to access their markets.

Difficulties shipping goods to other Palestinian areas and to Israel has also hampered trade. Palestinian trucks, for example, are not allowed to travel between towns in the West Bank and elsewhere. Goods must often be transferred from a truck on one side of a checkpoint to a truck on the other side. This process can take hours and frequently results in severe spoilage and destruction of food products. The curfews and blockades have thus forced many Palestinian businesses to shut their doors. In September 2003, the human rights group Amnesty International concluded that "closures, blockades, checkpoints, roadblocks, curfews, and other restrictions . . . have crippled the Palestinian economy. Unemployment and poverty have spiraled, malnutrition has emerged, anemia and other health problems have increased, and education has been negatively affected."[54]

Palestinian farmers have been especially hard hit by the restrictions.

A Palestinian woman curses Israeli troops for destroying her olive grove as they set up a checkpoint in the Gaza Strip.

Palestinian farms often lie on the Israeli side of barricades, making access to their own farmland nearly impossible for farmers. Crops are frequently lost or damaged because farmers cannot properly tend to them. Hebron's plum harvest, for example, dropped in value from $2.5 million in 2000 to $250,000 in 2001 because farmers were unable to ship the plums to other areas.

Vast groves of olive trees also lie dying. Palestinians have long tended their olive groves in the fertile soil of the West Bank and the Gaza Strip. During the last five years, however, the Israeli army destroyed thousands of acres of these trees, claiming that the olive groves pose a threat to Israeli security by providing hiding places for militants. Palestinians scoff at these explanations and accuse the Israelis of simply trying to undermine their economy. It has been estimated that the uprooting of just one olive tree costs a farmer more than seven hundred dollars in lost income.

In a further blow to the economy, Israeli air strikes and bombings have damaged hundreds of Palestinian businesses and farms. These attacks have destroyed vital water resources, electric generators, sewage and water treatment plants, hospitals, and telephone cables. These losses have negatively impacted sanitation, medical care, communication, and industry, and they have left many areas without power or water for weeks or months at a time. Palestinian industry has, in fact, come to a virtual standstill, leaving the Palestinian economy and much of the population in dire straits.

Unemployment, Poverty, and Food Shortages

Palestinian unemployment rates have skyrocketed because of the profound losses the economy has sustained. In turn, the standard of living has been dramatically reduced, resulting in extreme poverty. A case in point is Nabil Hani Ashur, a self-employed plumber living in Nablus. He is a widower with four children. His monthly salary has fallen in recent years by some 90 percent, making it nearly impossible for him to feed and support his family. Ashur's situation is common; indeed, unemployment affects nearly two out of three Palestinian families. The number of people living below the poverty level had, by July 2001, reached 57 percent in the West Bank and 80 percent in Gaza.

Food shortages are also common in the territories; in 2004 they affected 65 percent of all Palestinian households. These shortages are attributed to the lowered productivity of Palestinian farms and the travel restrictions and check points. Although the United Nations and other international organizations provide millions of dollars of food relief, these supplies are woefully inadequate to meet the Palestinians' needs.

Food shortages have led to widespread starvation and malnutrition among the population. Health problems such as anemia and vitamin deficiency have dramatically increased, especially among Palestinian children. The Palestinians see little hope that the food shortage situation will improve in the near future unless the Israelis ease travel

A worker for an Islamic charity distributes food to hungry Palestinian children in the West Bank. Food shortages affect more than half of Palestinian households.

restrictions and Palestinian farmers are once again allowed to adequately tend their fields.

The unemployment rate, the food shortages, the high rates of poverty, and the uncertain economic future of Palestinians have enormous bearing on the peace process. Although much of the misery and destruction has come about from efforts to curb terrorism, ironically the only thing that may reduce terrorism is improving the economic situation in the territories. As the director

of the World Bank in the occupied territories stated in 2002, "If the closures are lifted, the Palestinian economy will recover. If closures persist or intensify, the economy will unravel. Public services will break down. Unemployment and poverty rates will continue to climb. Helplessness, deprivation, and hatred will increase."[55]

Access to Health Care

The closures and restrictions have had a particularly negative impact on access to medical care. During the last four years, there have been many instances of Palestinians being unable to reach hospitals or other health care facilities because of Israeli roadblocks and curfews. During August 2002, for example, a study conducted by Johns Hopkins University revealed that nearly 50 percent of Palestinians needing kidney dialysis or chemotherapy for cancer were unable to reach a hospital providing such service. In fact, the West Bank and the Gaza Strip are totally cut off from East Jerusalem hospitals, many of which are the only ones that offer services for the chronically ill.

There are also numerous reports of patients who have died as a result of their inability to follow up with needed care. On April 10, 2002, for instance, a fifty-year-old kidney patient died in his home; a curfew had prevented him from receiving any kidney dialysis for several weeks. Only a few days earlier, a two-year-old child ran out of medicine that was needed to control her cerebral palsy and epilepsy. The family was unable to obtain her medication because of a curfew that prevented them from leaving their home. After a week without her medicine, the child's condition worsened and she began having seizures. The family asked the Israeli military for permission to take her to a nearby hospital. Because of Palestinian militant activity in the neighborhood, however, the Israelis initially denied the request. By the time Israeli soldiers finally allowed an ambulance to transport the child to the hospital, she was in critical condition and died shortly thereafter.

Even when curfews are lifted, Pales-

The Availability of Water Resources

The Israelis control over 80 percent of all water supplies in the occupied territories and dole out water to Palestinians. They often receive only small quantities of water, which are insufficient to meet their daily needs, much less water their crops. Palestinians complain that if they exceed their water limits or try to dig new wells, they are arrested and punished. Nearby Israeli settlers, however, have no such restrictions. They have unlimited access to water supplies and are free to water their lawns and crops, take frequent showers and baths, and wash their pets and cars. Osama, a Palestinian financial adviser, addresses this inequality with Wendy Pearlman, who quotes him in her book *Occupied Voices: Stories of Everyday Life from the Second Intifada*: "If you go to the refugee camps here, you'll see that they have no water to drink. A few meters away, the Israeli settlement has swimming pools."

The water quality available to the Palestinians is also of questionable content. Many must drink salty water, leaving the Palestinians with yellow teeth and kidney problems. According to a U.S. environmental assessment reported by the Middle East Policy Council, "Of 300 households surveyed in Nablus, not one had access to drinking water acceptable by international standards."

An Israeli soldier stops an ambulance carrying wounded Palestinians. Some injured or sick Palestinians have died during delays at Israeli security checkpoints.

tinian ambulances often run into problems. Mohammed, a Palestinian health care worker, describes one such problem: "Sometimes the ambulance picks up a patient and then gets stopped at a roadblock. The ambulance can't pass through, so nurses come and carry the patient on their shoulders until they reach the other side. Then a car takes him the rest of the way to the hospital. This happens a lot."[56]

While many human rights organizations have asked that restrictions on medical vehicles be lifted, the Israeli government refuses to change its policy. Because Palestinian terrorists have used ambulances to smuggle themselves and weapons into Israel, Israeli authorities are suspicious of any vehicle trying to cross into the Jewish state. Although the threat to Israel is real, innocent Palestinian citizens often pay the ultimate price for the delays and stoppages.

Palestinian Education

In the last few years, Israel has also applied restrictions and closures to many schools in the occupied territories,

A Palestinian teacher inspects her classroom, which was destroyed in an Israeli raid. While the Israelis purposely target some schools as training grounds for militants, they level others accidentally during raids.

claiming they are centers for Palestinian protesters and militants. In fact, there are several known colleges that are used by Hamas and other militant Palestinian groups to recruit young people to join the ranks of their terrorist organizations. Bir Zeit University in the West Bank is one such college and has been a frequent target of Israeli troops.

Night raids on both dormitories and student apartments are common, and classes are often disrupted or canceled. Likewise, faculty members are also subjected to raids, and a large proportion of the foreign faculty was expelled for refusing to sign a loyalty oath to Israel.

Another university that has felt the impact of Israeli scrutiny is Al-Quds

University, the only Palestinian university in Jerusalem. Long suspected of being a terrorist training center, the Israeli government closed the school in 2002 after finding evidence of ties with several radical and militant Palestinian groups. Israeli officials found countless university documents that clearly demonstrated that Al-Quds was supporting terrorism by sending financial aid to terrorists and their families and by training students in terrorist techniques. The college also glorified martyrdom; one class offered by the university was called the Wafa Idriss course in human rights and democracy, named after the first female Palestinian suicide bomber.

Israeli closures and curfews have also impacted Palestinian elementary and secondary schoolchildren. Many children are not able to attend school at all and are now being taught "underground." This practice started during the first intifada, when many Palestinian teachers decided to teach students in their homes after schools were shut down. This kind of teaching continues today, despite its being illegal under Israeli military law for more than ten Palestinians to meet together at one time. Other Palestinian children do not receive any education other than what can be taught to them at home by their parents.

For those Palestinians who have attended secondary schools, little incentive exists to continue their education at the college level. With unemployment rates in many places nearing 80 percent, thousands of college graduates are unable to find jobs. For example, Khaled, a nineteen-year-old Palestinian student, had a scholarship to study in Algeria but was refused an exit visa by Israeli authorities. He spoke to a reporter in January 2004: "I do not know what will happen in the future. How can I plan anything? Nothing is in my hands."[57] Many educational analysts agree that there is little future for thousands of Palestinian youths at this time.

A Letter to the World

In her book Occupied Voices: Stories of Everyday Life from the Second Intifada, *author Wendy Pearlman cites a letter sent by a Palestinian farmer to the people of the world.*

To whom it may concern:

Upon exhausting all other options and finding all doors closed, I am taking this opportunity to address myself to all those with mercy in their hearts. I am the sole provider for my twelve children. On the night of October 28, 2000, Israeli bulldozers razed my farm. They leveled olive trees, orange groves, and the eleven plastic greenhouses in which I grew tomatoes and green peppers. In addition to completely destroying my land, they demolished my house and all its belongings. . . .

Today, my family and I are living in a Red Cross camp. With neither work nor shelter, I am powerless. . . .

We hope in God Almighty and in those who find it within themselves to extend us a helping hand.

God bless you.

Sincerely,
Amer Jaber Barakat Daheer

A view of the wall that separates Israeli-held territory from the rest of the West Bank. The wall has divided families and separated farmers from their fields.

The Wall

While curfews and restrictions have nearly paralyzed certain sectors of Palestinian society, a new Israeli measure threatens to make the situation worse. In the early twenty-first century, the Israeli government responded to an increase in Palestinian suicide bombings by approving the construction of a wall along the Israeli border with the West Bank that is intended to physically prevent terrorists from entering Israel. The barrier will include a complex set of obstacles such as deep trenches, electric fences, and patrolling tanks. Palestinians will be required to cross the barrier at heavily monitored security gates in order to reach the rest of the West Bank and other areas, thus allowing the Israeli military and security forces to monitor all traffic into Israel. When it is completed, the wall is expected to be over four hundred miles long.

The construction of the wall is already negatively impacting Palestinian society. Sections of the blockade divide parts of the West Bank into small segments. In one community, for example, the wall surrounds the village on three sides. Palestinian farmers are unable to reach large parts of their olive groves and pastures, which lie on the other side of the barrier. Other communities are completely surrounded by the wall, cutting them off almost entirely from the outside world. The wall has added to the delays Palestinians endure while seeking medical care, visiting relatives, and tending to their businesses. To compound the situation, checkpoints are often closed for long periods, preventing any movement or travel.

The wall has also encroached on Palestinian land, some of which is the most fertile in the West Bank. Analysts say that more than 10 percent of the West Bank eventually will be annexed to Israel by this barrier. When completed, the wall will add more than forty Palestinian towns, home to more than three hundred thousand Palestinians, to Israel proper. This will further isolate many Palestinians from their countrymen, making the creation of a Palestinian state that much more difficult.

On January 11, 2004, Palestinian prime minister Ahmed Qureia urged the international community to put pressure on Israel to stop the construction of the wall. Qureia insists that the barrier is not a security measure but is instead an attempt by Israel to annex more land and create further economic problems for the Palestinian people. Despite international protests against the wall, there are no plans to have the barrier dismantled. Qureia urged Palestinians to continue their resistance to the wall and warned Israel that "the Palestinian people . . . will not accept this. . . . They will resist, they will struggle, they will remain steadfast until they get their legitimate national rights."[58]

Palestinians in Israel

Like their countrymen in the West Bank and the Gaza Strip, the 850,000 Palestinians who live in Israel struggle in their day-to-day lives. They, too, must contend with closures and restrictions of their freedom. The Israeli government, while promising equity to its Arab residents, has instead left many Palestinian neighborhoods in dire straits. These communities are frequently denied access to routine city services such as garbage removal and street repair. They are also very poor, but they are denied access to economic assistance programs. Abu Ghanem speaks of what it is like to live as a Palestinian in Israel: "Israel's [Palestinian] citizens [have been stripped] of dignity and power over their own lives. . . . I feel like a foreigner in my own country."[59]

Thousands of Palestinians in Israel are either unemployed or hold menial jobs. While a few Palestinians work in business, education, medicine, and law, the majority are forced to accept whatever kind of work is available. *National Geographic* journalist Don Belt elaborates on this situation: "Standing at the end of the hiring line behind thousands of [Jewish] immigrants from Russia and Ethiopia, [Palestinians] do the jobs nobody else wants to do. They clean the hotel rooms, build the houses, pump the gas, and bring in the crops. Many workers are unable to find adequate housing and are forced to sleep in . . . [empty market] stalls or cellars in the slums."[60]

Palestinian parents also complain that their children do not receive an adequate education in Israel. They say

Palestinian women take their final exams in a refugee camp where school facilities are inadequate and textbooks and supplies are difficult to obtain.

Palestinian schools are underfunded by the Israeli government, leaving many classrooms without textbooks and properly trained teachers. Many classes are held in old buildings with poor ventilation, no heat, and no running water. Palestinian schools are also subject to strict guidelines that prohibit the teaching of Palestinian history. If the teachers mention al-Nakba or the refugee situation, they are subject to the scrutiny of the Israeli Secret Service and risk arrest.

Furthermore, Palestinians complain that their Israeli neighbors often discriminate against them and bar them from stores, movie theaters, and restaurants. Palestinians who wish to travel outside the country are often denied passports and visas or delayed for months before being allowed to leave. Tired of feeling like second-class citizens, many Palestinians have left Israel for other parts of the world.

A Growing Sense of Hopelessness

The high rates of unemployment and poverty, along with the intrusive restrictions on their lives, have given rise to a growing sense of hopelessness among the Palestinians. Many wonder whether they will ever be able to adequately feed their families, find employment, or see friends and relatives in other parts of the region. Forced to rely on charity to meet many of their basic needs, feelings of desperation and powerlessness are on the rise.

Adding to their sense of despair is the humiliation that Palestinians often endure. Some Israelis do not respect them and treat them rudely. For example, Iman, a Palestinian university student, describes one experience with this kind of treatment: "My mother and I were out walking and a settler lady stopped us. . . . She spit on us and then just walked off. . . . We have to take all this and we're not supposed to say a thing. If we do, they can accuse us of trying to kill them."[61]

Today, Palestinians wonder if their situation will ever improve. They feel increasingly frustrated with their leaders, who have failed to achieve independence and peace. And they despair of a life in which violence, humiliation, and inequality continue. "Time and time again," author Wendy Pearlman writes, "Palestinians tell me they feel suspended between life and death."[62] Until there is a significant improvement in their lives, it is unlikely that these feelings will lift.

CHAPTER 6

Is There Hope for a Better Future?

The Palestinians are no closer today to their own independent homeland than they have been in the past. Violence in the West Bank and the Gaza Strip continues unabated, and Palestinian suicide bombings of Israeli targets have increased. Unemployment and poverty dominate Palestinian life in the occupied territories. Given these conditions, people all around the world wonder if peace is ever possible in this volatile area of the world. The Palestinians have many questions about their own future, the most prominent one being: Will there ever be an independent Palestine?

Palestinian Leadership

The Palestinian Authority (PA) led by Yasir Arafat does not seem able to settle this question. Many Palestinians, in fact, increasingly doubt whether Arafat and the PA will ever be able to achieve independence and peace for them. The PA has been unable to effect reforms to improve life in the territories. Nor has it been able to halt the construction of the wall Israel is building around the West Bank. Because of these lapses, support for Arafat has dropped to the lowest level since the 1970s.

Because many Palestinians feel disappointed by Arafat and the PA, they have increasingly turned to the militant group Hamas for direction and leadership. Many Palestinians respect Hamas militants for actively fighting for the nationalist goals that Arafat and the PA only talk about. Ron Pundak of the Peres Center for Peace in Tel Aviv explains Hamas's appeal: "Hamas is much stronger on the Palestinian street today because they are satisfying a gut desire for revenge. They are the heroes of the day."[63]

Palestinian women carry flags showing support for Hamas. Known for its terrorist activities, Hamas has also worked to obtain jobs, medicine, and food for those in need.

Although Hamas sponsors terrorism, the group has also gained supporters because it has enacted many social service programs that are widely used by Palestinians. Hamas's social services branch has constructed a wide-ranging social network that has been successful in finding people housing, jobs, loans, medicine, and food. The movement has also funded programs in education, family aid, orphan care, and sports. It runs an extensive distribution program that provides food, clothing, medicine, and household items for the needy. It also builds mosques, health clinics, and libraries.

These efforts are much appreciated by unemployed and poverty-stricken Palestinians, who have not been as significantly helped by the Palestinian Authority. Terrorist expert Magnus Ranstorp explains Hamas's success in this area: "Unlike Arafat's Palestinian Authority, which is rife with corruption . . . Hamas has developed a reputation for honesty and trustworthiness. The group has . . . generally been able to provide help to Palestinians at a time when the Palestinian Authority is powerless."[64] Hama's strength is most apparent in the Gaza Strip, the region that has seen the most violence in the last four years. It is here where Hamas is beginning to play an active political role; little, in fact, is done in Gaza without the consent of Hamas officials. According to many political analysts and world leaders, the growing popularity of Hamas is a massive obstacle to peace. Hamas is viewed as an ever-growing threat to Israel because it perpetually calls for Israel's destruction and continually sends suicide bombers into the country toward that end. That the group enjoys increasing popularity among Palestinians does not bode well for the peace process, which relies on moderate voices on both sides to make compromises on which a lasting peace will rest.

The Israeli Settlements

The presence of Israeli settlements in the occupied territories has long been a huge obstacle to the peace process. The Palestinians bitterly resent the nearly two hundred thousand Israelis who live in settlements in the West Bank and the Gaza Strip. Their presence makes it infinitely more difficult for a Palestinian state to become a reality because the Israeli settlers have put roots down in the land that might eventually become part of that state. The Israeli settlers, however, adamantly assert their right to live on land they consider to be part

of Israel, and they vehemently resist all efforts by the Israeli government to make them move. Indeed, the Israeli army has often clashed with its own countrymen while acting on orders by the government to dismantle settlements.

Even the Israeli government's willingness to dismantle settlements has snagged the peace process, however. On

Under Prime Minister Ariel Sharon, Israel began a slow dismantling of some of the West Bank settlements in 2003.

the few occasions when Israel has been willing to remove settlements, it has announced its intention to do so unilaterally, without consulting Palestinian leaders. Toward the end of 2003, for example, Israeli prime minister Ariel Sharon announced his country's intention to withdraw many of its settlements from the West Bank and the Gaza Strip. Although the Palestinians have for years demanded exactly such a withdrawal, Palestinian leaders were infuriated that they were not consulted about how this process would be carried out. Any decision about the future of Palestine that does not include Palestinian participation is totally unacceptable and illegitimate to Palestinian leaders. Their dismay was heightened when they learned that, far from removing all settlements, Israel intended only a partial withdrawal. The issue of Israeli settlements is very sensitive and will likely remain a key stumbling block to peace in the future.

Israel's Policy of Targeted Assassinations

Yet another obstacle to peace is the controversial Israeli policy of assassinating Palestinian terrorist leaders. The Israeli government routinely targets leading militants of groups such as Hamas for assassination in an attempt to stamp out terrorism. However, the assassination of terrorist leaders, who enjoy much respect and prestige among Palestinians, usually has the opposite effect. For example, when Hamas leader Sheik Ahmed Yassin was assassinated on March 21, 2004, Israel inadvertently unleashed the largest wave of violence in the occupied territories in recent years.

Israeli military helicopters fired three missiles at the Hamas leader, his bodyguards, and dozens of other Palestinians as they left a mosque in Gaza. Yassin, who had approved and initiated hundreds of terrorist attacks against Israeli targets, was killed along with seven others. Israeli spokeswoman Brigadier General Ruth Yarm issued a statement on behalf of the Israeli government: "The Israeli air force this morning killed the mastermind of all evil, Ahmed Yassin, who was a preacher of death."[65]

While the Israelis celebrated the death of the notorious terrorist, Hamas supporters and other Palestinians mourned the loss of a beloved leader. At Yassin's funeral, which was well attended by thousands of mourners, Palestinian flags waved and gunfire filled the air. Masked gunmen from Hamas marched with militants from other terrorist groups, chanting, "death to Israel" and "death to America." Ismail Haniyeh, a Hamas official and close associate of Yassin, spoke for the masses: "Words cannot describe the emotion of anger and hate inside our hearts."[66] He vowed revenge on Israel for the assassination of the Hamas leader.

Following the assassination, Abdel Aziz Rantisi, a hard-liner within the Hamas organization, was chosen to succeed Yassin. Rantisi, a fifty-year-old pediatrician, advocated increasing the number of attacks on Israel and steadfastly refused to compromise with the Palestinian Authority and Yasir Arafat.

Sheik Ahmed Yassin

Sheik Ahmed Yassin was the spiritual leader of Hamas. One of the most infamous terrorists in the Middle East, he was responsible for hundreds of terrorist attacks against Israelis.

As a young man, Yassin fell on his head while doing gymnastics and was partially paralyzed. Despite this disability, he pursued his education, obtained a degree, and began working as a teacher in a Palestinian elementary school. During this time, he founded al-Mojamaa al-Islami, a welfare charity also known as the Islamic Society. He was arrested by Israeli officials in 1983 for conspiring to form

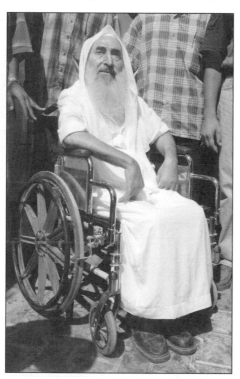

a military group, and he was released two years later during a prisoner exchange. In 1987, during the first intifada, he founded Hamas and vowed to use terrorism to secure Palestinian independence.

Yassin was imprisoned for the second time by the Israelis in 1991. While in jail, he was further injured, rendering him a quadriplegic. Released in October 1997, Yassin led Hamas from his wheelchair and home in Gaza City, where he ordered Palestinian suicide bombers to carry out hundreds of attacks inside Israel. He was assassinated in March 2004.

Hamas leader Sheik Ahmed Yassin addresses the media in Gaza a few months before Israeli forces assassinated him, using missiles fired from helicopters.

As he accepted the leadership of Hamas, Rantisi pledged to continue Yassin's policy of terror and suicide bombings: "We will fight them until the liberation of Palestine, the whole of Palestine."[67] He followed his speech by ordering Hamas militants in Gaza to increase the level of violence and launch more suicide missions on Israeli targets. Less than a month later, Rantisi was also assassinated by the Israeli army.

Many world leaders, along with the United Nations, immediately condemned Israel's action, claiming that the assassinations impede any chance of peace in the region. Many political analysts and journalists also question the effectiveness of Israel's targeted assassination policy. For example, Amy Wilentz of the *Los Angeles Times* wrote:

Hamas fighters attend the funeral of Sheik Ahmed Yassin. Following the death of their spiritual leader, many in Hamas vowed vengeance against Israel.

"[Israeli prime minister Ariel] Sharon has earned the condemnation of almost the entire world . . . [and in the process] he's created the ultimate Palestinian martyr."[68] Many followers of the Israeli-Palestinian conflict agree that assassinating Hamas leaders will neither stop the suicide bombings nor change Hamas policies. *Time* journalist Johanna McGeary explains, "Few expect that the killing of Yassin will do anything to

deter Hamas, which derives most of its power not from individual leaders but from the appeal of its ideas to a generation of despairing Palestinians."[69]

The "Road Map" to Peace

Israel's unilateral decision making, the assassination of Hamas leaders, the continued suicide bombings, and the growing Palestinian criticism of the PA have all negatively impacted a peace process known as the "road map." The road map is sponsored by the United States, Russia, the European Union, and the United Nations. This peace plan was created to lead the Palestinians and the Israelis through various negotiations, resulting in an equitable peace. The road map includes provisions that call for the Palestinians to disarm the militant groups and require the Israeli government to dismantle and remove unauthorized settlements from the West Bank and Gaza. World leaders hoped that these moves would lead to the establishment of a Palestinian state by 2005.

However, as of May 2004 neither side had fulfilled any of the required obligations. Israeli leaders repeatedly assert that the continued suicide bombings by Hamas and other groups prevent their government from negotiating a final settlement. Prime Minister Sharon has stated the Israeli position clearly: "As long as terror continues, as long as violence continues, as long as their terrible incitement continues, there will be no progress. There will be no peace with terror."[70]

The Palestinians have been just as adamant in their stance toward Israel. Condemning the targeted assassinations and Israel's announcement that many West Bank settlements will not be dismantled, Palestinian leaders charge Israel with impeding the peace process. Arafat stresses that any effective peace plan must include Israeli military withdrawal from all Palestinian land. He also insists on the return of any Palestinian land confiscated during the building of the wall. Majid, a Palestinian American, explains the Palestinian position on this issue: "I think Palestinians feel that they're losing every single day more and more of their land. . . . Unless they have incentive, I don't feel that they have basically any reason to stop fighting."[71]

Rapidly deteriorating economic conditions among the Palestinians also imperil the road map to peace. With little hope of economic improvement, Palestinians have become exasperated with the stalled peace talks. Palestinian Alexandra Avakian speaks passionately about this issue: "If the world wants peace in the Middle East," she states, "they should help Arafat bring jobs and industry to Gaza and allow these people to work. Because if they are working they're going to be thinking a lot less about violent solutions."[72] An immediate improvement in the quality of the Palestinians' day-to-day living is a necessity, the Palestinians say, for any negotiations to succeed.

The United States, Russia, the European Union, and the United Nations are also exhausted by the endless cycle of violence and the seemingly impossible task of finding compromises that will satisfy both sides. While the Europeans want to move forward and put the road map into effect, the United States and Israel have publicly indicated that they will wait until Yasir Arafat has been removed from power before finalizing any agreement. They cite Arafat as an obstacle to peace due to his apparent unwillingness or inability to rein in terrorists. U.S. president George W. Bush has also demanded that Hamas be

The Assassination of Another Hamas Leader

On April 17, 2004, less than a month after Sheik Ahmed Yassin was assassinated, new Hamas leader Abdel Aziz Rantisi was also killed. Rantisi had been one of the most outspoken members of that organization, advocating the destruction of Israel by any means necessary. He frequently condemned Yasir Arafat for his willingness to negotiate with the Israelis for peace. At the time of his death, Rantisi was negotiating with other Palestinian officials to take over the political administration of the Gaza Strip after the expected Israeli pullout sometime in 2005.

Rantisi had skirted death before and had been wounded in June 2003 when Israeli helicopters fired missiles toward his car. Nearly a year later, the Israelis accomplished their goal when helicopters fired two missiles into a white sedan, killing Rantisi and two others, including his son. As news of Rantisi's death spread through Gaza, tens of thousands of furious Palestinians swarmed to the streets, vowing revenge. Following Rantisi's death, Hamas appointed a new chief in the Gaza Strip but refused to reveal his identity, lest he, too, face assassination.

Hamas supporters carry the body of Abdel Aziz Rantisi to his home in Gaza for burial.

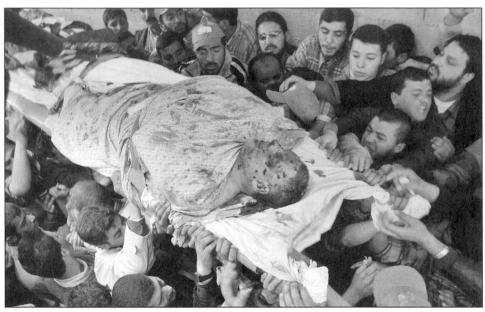

dismantled and insists that Arafat take charge of eliminating the militant group. In the meantime, the road map and the peace process remain stalled and unlikely to be jumpstarted in the near future.

Joint Efforts Toward Peace

While there is still a great deal of distrust and animosity between the Palestinians and the Israelis, many individuals and groups on both sides of the conflict are finding ways to work toward peace together. They hope that by working as a team they can lessen the tension between their peoples. Their joint efforts give hope to many people that the seemingly overwhelming obstacles to peace can be overcome. Through unity and cooperation, it is hoped the Israelis and the Palestinians can find common ground to move forward into a less-violent future.

Two such groups, the Israeli Parents' Circle and the Palestinian National Movement for Change, have been working together to promote peace between Israelis and Palestinians. Representatives from these groups met with members of the U.S. Congress in 2002 and made an appeal to the American government to take action to end the long conflict. In a powerful demonstration near the United Nations complex in New York, the two groups stood together before a thousand mock coffins representing Israelis and Palestinians who have died since 2000. They pleaded with the United States and the United Nations to use their influence to stop the violence. They hoped their symbolic display would heighten world awareness of the devastation the long conflict has caused.

Several members of the joint delegation made personal pleas to the American people and government. Yitzhak Frankenthal, an Israeli businessman who lost his son to Muslim extremists in 1994, said: "Hatred will not bring Arik back; revenge will not bring Arik back. Only reconciliation, tolerance, and peace will . . . give a chance to my other children to stay alive."[73] His Part-

ner in peace, Palestinian Salameh Musa Tomeizi, believes the same thing, despite having lost his son and two nephews to Israeli extremists. "All of us," Tomeizi said, "Palestinians and Israelis, want to live together in two states with good cooperation."[74] Their groups continue to search for ways to end the violence and achieve peace in the Holy Land.

Religious groups are also taking part in the effort to improve the relationship between Palestinians and Israelis and dissolve the current atmosphere of hate and distrust. In early December 2003, for instance, thirty-two prominent Christian, Jewish, and Muslim leaders announced the formation of the National Interreligious Leadership Initiative for Peace, which will work to end the religious conflicts that divide the Palestinians and the Israelis. The group recommends regular meetings between religious representatives from all sectors of faith. It also pleads with Palestinian leaders to stop the suicide bombings and begs the Israeli government to end the destructive retaliatory incursions.

Even more important than the organizations, perhaps, are the large numbers of Israeli and Palestinian people who work on their own to promote peace and understanding between the two peoples. During National Geographic journalist Tad Szulc's visit to the Middle East in the mid-1990s, he spoke with a number of individuals, both Israeli and Palestinian, who gave him hope that peace would eventually prevail. "Even more touching," he writes, "and perhaps more important, are the nameless individuals—Palestinians and Israelis, who somehow maintain their friendships, performing small acts of kindness for one another."[75] Simple things such as an Israeli driving his Palestinian friend to the hospital or a Palestinian helping an elderly Jewish neighbor tend his garden keep the hopes of many alive that there is a chance for peace.

These individual and group efforts have earned high praise from many international and regional organizations. Richard Fee, a member of the International Christian Committee that provides emergency food to Palestinian villages, speaks of the impact these groups are having:

Throughout my visit to the Holy Land . . . I saw that, despite the incredible sadness of this land, many people on both sides have come to understand that violence is not a solution. . . . We met Palestinians and Israelis working together against racism and discrimination. We met Israelis and Palestinians working together to help Palestinian farmers bring in the olive harvest.[76]

Is There a Future for the Palestinians?

Despite the many obstacles that stand in the way of independence, many Palestinians hold onto their resolve for a better future. Azza, a Palestinian filmmaker, talks with determination about his hopes: "I believe we're going to win in the end just because we're here, and we're staying, and they can't get rid of us. No system like that has been able to survive."[77]

Many ordinary Palestinians are not consumed with thoughts of revenge and retaliation for the Israelis. Rather, they are absorbed in a struggle to feed

During a protest in New York, an Israeli man and Palestinian woman talk, surrounded by coffins symbolizing recent casualties in the Israeli-Palestinian conflict.

A Palestinian Call for Peace

More than fifty Palestinians took out a full-page advertisement in the June 19, 2002, edition of the Arabic language newspaper Al-Quds, imploring their countrymen to abandon violent tactics. The complete ad can be found on the Independent Media Review Analysis Web site.

Due to the dangerous situation under which the Palestinian people are living and as part of our national responsibility, we, the undersigned, seek to wish that those who stand behind the military operations targeting civilians in Israel reconsider their policy and refrain from recruiting young Palestinians for the purpose of mounting military attacks. . . .

We believe that military operations do not contribute to the development or accomplishment of our national project that calls for freedom and independence. On the contrary, the operations increase the number of the enemies of peace on the Israeli side and offer excuses to the government of Israel, headed by [Prime Minister Ariel] Sharon, to escalate its military aggression against Palestinian children and the elderly, and against Palestinian cities and villages. The Israeli aggression also targets our accomplishments, aspirations and national project.

The positive and negative features of a military operation are defined by whether political goals are achieved and not by the operations as a standard unto themselves. Therefore there is a need for the people involved in the military operations to reconsider their actions, which we believe only heightens tension between the Palestinians and Israelis and drives them toward war and destruction, which have no logical, human or political rationale.

their families from one day to the next. What they want, they say, is to be able to control their own lives, travel freely, reunite with their extended families, and live in freedom. They want to be able to provide financially for their families and send their children to school in safety. Ibrahim, a twenty-year-old Palestinian expressed this desire when he said. "If I get married and have children, I want my kids to have a life. A life without fear. A life that allows you to put your head on the pillow at night and not be afraid that you'll be killed before you wake up."[78]

Many Palestinians are also realistic enough to understand that peace will not come easily. With the Palestinian militants unwilling to stop the violence until Israel withdraws its troops, and the Israelis unwilling to withdraw until the terrorism stops, the peace process is at an impasse. Palestinians, however, continue to hope for the best and work toward that end, believing that one day in the future they will live in an independent Palestine.

NOTES

Introduction:
Who Are the Palestinians?

1. Jimmy Carter, *The Blood of Abraham: Insights into the Middle East.* Boston: Houghton Mifflin, 1985, p. 1.
2. *Peace Encyclopedia*, "Palestinians," www.yahoodi.com/peace/palestinians.html.
3. Tad Szulc, "Who Are the Palestinians?" *National Geographic*, June 1992, p. 92.
4. David Lamb, *The Arabs.* New York: Vintage, 2002, p. 210.

Chapter 1:
Al-Nakba: The Catastrophe

5. Passport Palestine, "The Exchange of Letters," www.passportpalestine.com/library/mcmanintro.htm.
6. Quoted in Daniel C. Diller, ed., *The Middle East.* Washington, DC: Congressional Quarterly, 1994, p. 10.
7. Michael J. Cohen, *The Origins and Evolution of the Arab-Zionist Conflict.* Berkeley: University of California Press, 1987, p. 89.
8. Karen Armstrong, *Jerusalem: One City, Three Faiths.* New York: Alfred A. Knopf, 1996, p. 385.
9. Helena Cobban, *The Palestine Liberation Organization.* London: Cambridge University Press, 1984, p. 7.
10. Quoted in Cohen, *The Origins and Evolution of the Arab-Zionist Conflict*, p. 163.
11. Cohen, *The Origins and Evolution of the Arab-Zionist Conflict*, p. 106.
12. Quoted in Laurel Holliday, *Children of Israel, Children of Palestine.* New York: Pocket, 1998, p. 236.
13. Quoted in Jerome Slater, "What Went Wrong?" *Academy of Political Science*, 2001.
14. Quoted in Holliday, *Children of Israel, Children of Palestine*, p. 208.
15. Quoted in Holliday, *Children of Israel, Children of Palestine*, p. 208.
16. Quoted in David K. Shipler, *Arab and Jew: Wounded Spirits in a Promised Land.* New York: Times, 1986, p. 40.
17. Quoted in Holliday, *Children of Israel, Children of Palestine*, p. 74.

Chapter 2: The Growth of Palestinian Nationalism

18. *Peace Encyclopedia*, "Refugees," www.yahoodi.com/peace/refugees.html.

19. *National Geographic*, "The Gaza Strip: Interview with Alexandra Avakian," 1996. www.nationalgeographic.com/gaza/b003.html.

20. Quoted in Holliday, *Children of Israel, Children of Palestine*, p. 280.

21. Adina Friedman, "Unraveling the Right of Return," *Center for Refugee Studies*, 2003.

22. Cobban, *The Palestine Liberation Organization*, p. 37.

23. Quoted in Julian Becker, *The PLO: The Rise and Fall of the Palestine Liberation Organization*. New York: St. Martin's, 1984, p. 67.

24. Quoted in Lamb, *The Arabs*, p. 224.

25. Quoted in Becker, *The PLO*, p. 193.

26. Quoted in Cobban, *The Palestine Liberation Organization*, p. 62.

27. Quoted in Lamb, *The Arabs*, p. 201.

28. Quoted in Wendy Pearlman, *Occupied Voices: Stories of Everyday Life from the Second Intifada*. New York: Nation, 2003 p. 7.

Chapter 3: The Palestinian Authority

29. Lamb, *The Arabs*, p. 232.

30. Madeleine Albright, *Madam Secretary*. New York: Miramax, 2003, p. 296.

31. Quoted in Friedman, "Unraveling the Right of Return."

32. Shipler, *Arab and Jew*, p. 33.

33. Albright, *Madam Secretary*, p. 289.

34. Quoted in Pearlman, *Occupied Voices*, p. 141.

35. Erika Waak, "Violence Among the Palestinians," *Humanist*, 2003.

36. John Ward Anderson and Molly Moore, "Palestinian Authority Broke and in Disarray," *Washington Post*, March 1, 2004.

Chapter 4: Perpetrators and Victims

37. Quoted in Stephen Zunes, "The United States and the Breakdown of the Israeli-Palestinian Peace Process," *Middle East Policy Council*, 2001.

38. Armstrong, *Jerusalem*, p. 416.

39. Quoted in *Dallas Morning News*, "Hamas Militants Are Heroic Martyrs," 2001.

40. Quoted in Holliday, *Children of Israel, Children of Palestine*, p. 338.

41. Quoted in Associated Press, "Palestinian Bomber Becomes First Woman," January 14, 2004.

42. Quoted in Lamb, *The Arabs*, p. 90.

43. Quoted in Zunes, "The United States and the Breakdown of the Israeli-Palestinian Peace Process."

44. Lamb, *The Arabs*, p. 87.

45. Quoted in *National Geographic*, "The Gaza Strip."

46. Quoted in Holliday, *Children of Israel, Children of Palestine*, p. 297.

47. Quoted in Holliday, *Children of Israel, Children of Palestine*, p. 289.

48. Quoted in Muna Hamzeh-Muhaisen, "Who Will Protect the Children of Aida Refugee Camp?" *Palestine Report*, November 21, 1997. www.jmcc.org/media/report/97/Nov/3.htm#one.

49. Quoted in Pearlman, *Occupied Voices*, p. 85.

50. Johanna McGeary, "Inside Hamas," *Time*, April 5, 2004, p. 51.

Chapter 5: Life in the West Bank and the Gaza Strip

51. Quoted in Pearlman, *Occupied Voices*, p. 9.

52. Quoted in Amnesty USA, "Israel/Occupied Territories: Surviving Under Siege," September 8, 2003. www.amnestyusa.org/countries/israel_and_occupied_territories/index.do.

53. Quoted in *National Geographic*, "The Gaza Strip."

54. Quoted in Amnesty USA, "Israel/Occupied Territories."

55. Quoted in Pearlman, *Occupied Voices*, p. 182.

56. Quoted in Pearlman, *Occupied Voices*, p. 97.

57. Quoted in Melissa, "Diaries: Arab and Jew: Being Young in a Troubled Land," *Electronic Intifada*, January 7, 2004. http://electronicintifada.net/v2/article2331.shtml.

58. Quoted in Associated Press, "Sharon Says," January 12, 2004.

59. Quoted in Don Belt, "Living in the Shadow of Peace," *National Geographic*, June 1995, p. 79.

60. Belt, "Living in the Shadow of Peace," p. 81.

61. Pearlman, *Occupied Voices*, p. 170.

62. Pearlman, *Occupied Voices*, p. 245.

Chapter 6: Is There Hope for a Better Future?

63. Quoted in *Dallas Morning News*, "Hamas Militants Are Heroic Martyrs."

64. Quoted in *Dallas Morning News*, "Hamas Militants Are Heroic Martyrs."

65. Quoted in Ibrahim Barzak, "Hamas Founder Sheik Ahmed Yassin Assassinated," *AOL News*, March 21, 2004. http://aolsvc.news.aol.com/news/article.adp?id=20040321225109990002.

66. Quoted in Barzak, "Hamas Founder Sheik Ahmed Yassin Assassinated."

67. Quoted in *Week*, "Palestinians Vow Revenge for Slain Hamas Leader," April 2, 2004.

68. *Week*, "Palestinians Vow Revenge for Slain Hamas Leader."

69. McGeary, "Inside Hamas," p. 47.

70. Quoted in Justin Huggler, "Road Map for Peace," *Independent London*, June 21, 2003.

71. Quoted in Steve Innskeep, "President Bush's Plan," *NPR: Talk of the Nation*, June 25, 2002.

72. Quoted in *National Geographic*, "The Gaza Strip."

73. Quoted in Caryle Murphy, "United in Grief, Israelis, Palestinians in D.C.," *Washington Post*, March 21, 2002.

74. Quoted in Murphy, "United in Grief, Israelis, Palestinians in D.C."

75. Szulc, "Who Are the Palestinians?" p. 108

76. Richard Fee, "Seeking Peace in the Middle East," *Presbyterian Record*, November 1, 2002.

77. Quoted in Pearlman, *Occupied Voices*, p. 151.

78. Quoted in Pearlman, *Occupied Voices*, p. 131.

FOR FURTHER READING

Books

Frederick Fisher, *Israel*. Milwaukee: Gareth Stevens, 2000. The author presents a history of Israel and focuses on the Arab-Israeli conflict.

Martin Hintz and Stephen Hintz, *Israel*. New York: Children's Press, 1999. An overall look at the state of Israel, with several chapters devoted to the conflict with the Palestinians.

Carolyn J. Long, *The Middle East in Search of Peace*. Brookfield, CT: Millbrook, 1994. This excellent book offers abundant information about the conflict in the Middle East.

Elsa Marsten, *Lebanon*. New York: Dillon, 1994. Details the Israeli invasion of Lebanon and the use of that country by the Palestine Liberation Organization.

Web Sites

Intifada 2000, "Dear Diary," Muna Hamzeh Muhaisen (http://xii.net. intifada/2000/deardiary/dear diary.toc.htm). This Web site contains a diary entry from a person living in the occupied territories. It offers a glimpse of life there.

Save the Children, "Eye to Eye: Meet Some Children" (www.savethechildren. org.uk/eyetoeye/visit/meet.html). This Web site connects the reader to the stories of several children living in the occupied territories.

WORKS CONSULTED

Books

Madeleine Albright, *Madam Secretary*. New York: Miramax, 2003. Memoirs of the former secretary of state under President Bill Clinton. Several sections focus on the conflict in the Middle East, including the various Israeli-Palestinian peace conferences held in the late 1990s.

Karen Armstrong, *Jerusalem: One City, Three Faiths*. New York: Alfred A. Knopf, 1996. Focuses on the city of Jerusalem, which is a holy place for Jews, Muslims, and Christians.

Julian Becker, *The PLO: The Rise and Fall of the Palestine Liberation Organization*. New York: St. Martin's, 1984. Explains the structures, aims, tactics, and the role of the Palestine Liberation Organization in the Middle East and in world politics.

Douglas Brinkley, *The Unfinished Presidency*. New York: Penguin, 1998. This award-winning historian writes of former president Jimmy Carter's life after he left office. Major portions of the book focus on Carter's efforts to bring peace to the Middle East.

Caleb Carr, *The Lessons of Terror*. New York: Random House, 2002. This military historian examines terrorism throughout history, including the international terrorism of today. There is an excellent chapter on the use of terrorism in the conflict between the Israelis and the Palestinians.

Jimmy Carter, *The Blood of Abraham: Insights into the Middle East*. Boston: Houghton Mifflin, 1985. Since he took office in 1977, this former American president has tirelessly pursued the question of peace in the Middle East. In this book, he offers readers an overview of the political, religious, and ethnic conflicts that have divided the Middle East.

Noam Chomsky, *The Fateful Triangle: The United States, Israel, and the Palestinians*. Boston: South End, 1983. Explores the development of Israel's relationship with the United States as well as its impact on the Palestinians.

Helena Cobban, *The Palestine Liberation Organization*. London: Cambridge University Press, 1984. A former

Middle East correspondent examines the Palestine Liberation Organization.

Michael J. Cohen, *The Origins and Evolution of the Arab-Zionist Conflict*. Berkeley and Los Angeles: University of California Press, 1987. Focuses primarily on the period before 1948, when Great Britain ruled Palestine.

Daniel C. Diller, ed., *The Middle East*. Washington, DC: Congressional Quarterly, 1994. Traces the history, participants, and issues involved in the Middle East conflict.

Laurel Holliday, *Children of Israel, Children of Palestine*. New York: Pocket, 1998. The author recounts the stories of both Palestinians and Israelis who grew up during the years of turmoil following Israel's independence in 1948.

David Lamb, *The Arabs*. New York: Vintage, 2002. This excellent book presents a portrait of the Arab world. Several chapters are devoted to Palestinian issues.

Wendy Pearlman, *Occupied Voices: Stories of Everyday Life from the Second Intifada*. New York: Nation, 2003. The author, a young Jewish woman from the United States, recounts her travels in the West Bank and the Gaza Strip and her interviews with Palestinian refugees.

David K. Shipler, *Arab and Jew: Wounded Spirits in a Promised Land*. New York: Times, 1986. Examines the relationships between Arabs and Jews since the formation of the state of Israel in 1948.

Periodicals

Saud Abu-Ramadan, "Yassin: Hamas Founder and Spiritual Leader," United Press International, September 8, 2003.

Agence France Presse English, "Arafat Says Sharon Does Not Want Peace," January 6, 2004.

———, "Israel Presses Deadly Raid on Gaza," October 11, 2003.

John Ward Anderson and Molly Moore, "Palestinian Authority Broke and in Disarray," *Washington Post*, March 1, 2004.

Associated Press, "Israelis Seize $6.7 Million from Palestinians," *Dayton Daily News*, February 26, 2004.

———, "Palestinian Bomber Becomes First Woman," January 14, 2004.

———, "Sharon Says," January 12, 2004.

Associated Press Worldstream, "Arafat Remains in Charge," June 5, 2003.

Ibrahim Barzak, "Israeli Raid Kills Fourteen Palestinians," *Dayton Daily News*, March 8, 2004.

Don Belt, "Living in the Shadow of Peace," *National Geographic*, June 1995.

Noam Chomsky, "A Wall as a Weapon," *Dayton Daily News*, February 29, 2004.

Hillel Cohen, "Land, Memory, and Identity: The Palestinian Internal Refugees in Israel," *Refuge*, February 1, 2003.

Dallas Morning News, "Hamas Militants Are Heroic Martyrs," 2001.

Richard Fee, "Seeking Peace in the Middle East," *Presbyterian Record*, November 1, 2002.

Adina Friedman, "Unraveling the Right of Return," *Center for Refugee Studies*, 2003.

Matthew Gutman, "Fatah's Strength Said Rapidly Declining," *Jerusalem Post*, November 21, 2002.

Lee Hockstader, "Palestinians Hail a Heroine," *Washington Post*, January 31, 2002.

Stacy Howlett, "Palestinian Private Property Rights in Israel and the Occupied Territories," *Vanderbilt University School of Law Abstract*, 2001.

Justin Huggler, "Road Map for Peace," *Independent London*, June 21, 2003.

Lara Jamjoun, "The Effects of Israeli Violence," *Crime and Social Justice Association*, 2002.

Laura King, "Palestinian Refugee Camps Have Become Conflict's Deadliest Battlegrounds," *AP Worldstream*, April 9, 2002.

Uzi Landau, "Al-Quds U. and the Rule of Law," *Jerusalem Post*, July 17, 2002.

Peter Lippman, "As Peace Initiatives Come and Go," *Washington Report on Middle East Affairs*, March 1, 2004.

Rachelle Marshall, "Sharon Offers the Palestinians a Prison Camp," *Washington Report on Middle East Affairs*, March 1, 2004.

Johanna McGeary, "Inside Hamas," *Time*, April 5, 2004.

Middle East Policy Council, "Ending the Palestinian Economy," 2002.

Caryle Murphy, "United in Grief, Israelis, Palestinians in D.C.," *Washington Post*, March 21, 2002.

Craig Nelson, "Israelis Kill Hamas Co-Founder," *Dayton Daily News*, April 18, 2004.

Ravi Nessman, "Israel Steps Up Offensive in Gaza," *Dayton Daily News*, March 18, 2004.

Margot Patterson, "Christians in the Crossfire," *National Catholic Reporter*, May 10, 2002.

Matt Rees, "Prepare to Evacuate," *Time*, April 12, 2004.

Barry Schweid, "Bush Gives Support to Courageous Sharon Plan for Peace Settlement," *Dayton Daily News*, April 15, 2004.

Charmaine Seitz, "Palestinian Women," *Contemporary Women's Issues Database*, February 1, 1999.

Jerome Slater, "What Went Wrong?" *Academy of Political Science*, 2001.

Tad Szulc, "Who Are the Palestinians?" *National Geographic*, June 1992.

Ritu Upadhyay, "A Fragile Peace Is Torn Apart," *Time for Kids*, October 20, 2000.

Erika Waak, "Violence Among the Palestinians," *Humanist*, 2003.

Week, "How They See Us: Bush Sold Out the Palestinians," April 30, 2004.

———, "Israel to Withdraw from Gaza," February 13, 2004.

———, "Israel: Was It Right to Kill the Sheikh?" April 9, 2004.

———, "Palestinians Vow Revenge for Slain Hamas Leader," April 2, 2004.

Stephen Zunes, "The United States and the Breakdown of the Israeli-

Palestinian Peace Process," *Middle East Policy Council*, 2001.

Radio Broadcast Transcripts

Neil Conan, "Future of Yasser Arafat," *NPR: Talk of the Nation*, December 17, 2001.

Bob Edwards, "Vanishing Importance of the PA," *NPR: Morning Edition*, February 25, 2004.

Steve Innskeep, "President Bush's Plan," *NPR: Talk of the Nation*, June 25, 2002.

Internet Sources

Amnesty USA, "Israel/Occupied Territories: Surviving Under Siege," September 8, 2003. www.amnestyusa.org/countries/israel_and_occupied_territories/index.do.

Ibrahim Barzak, "Hamas Founder Sheik Ahmed Yassin Assassinated," *AOL News*, March 21, 2004. http://aolsvc.news.aol.com/news/article.adp?id-20040321225109990002.

Electronic Intifada, "Development: 193 Million in Relief Needed," January 13, 2003. http://electronicintifada.net/v2/article2257.shtml.

———, "Human Rights," January 17, 2004. http://electronicintifada.net/v2/article2355.shtml.

———, "Human Rights: Weekly Report on Human Rights' Violations," January 15, 2004. http://electronicintifada.net/v2/article2351.shtml.

Muna Hamzeh-Muhaisen, "Dear Diary," *Intifada 2000*. http://xii.net/intifada/2000/deardiary/dear-diary.toc.htm.

———, "Who Will Protect the Children of Aida Refugee Camp?" *Pales-tine Report*, November 21, 1997. www.jmcc.org/media/report/97/Nov/3.htm#one.

Independent Media Review Analysis, "English Translation of *Al Quds* Ad Against Targeting Civilians," June 20, 2002. www.imra.org.il/story.php3?id=12560.

Melissa, "Diaries: Arab and Jew: Being Young in a Troubled Land," *Electronic Intifada*, January 7, 2004. http://electronicintifada.net/v2/article2331.shtml.

Mid East Web, "Hamas Charter," www.mideastweb.org/hamas.htm.

National Geographic, "The Gaza Strip: Interview with Alexandra Avakian," 1996. www.nationalgeographic.com/gaza/b003.html.

Palestinian Women Martyrs, "Palestinian Women Martyrs Against the Israeli Occupation," http://aztlan.net/women_martyrs.htm.

Passport Palestine, "The Exchange of Letters," www.passportpalestine.com/library/mcmanintro.htm.

Peace Encyclopedia, "Palestinians," www.yahoodi.com/peace/palestinians.html.

———, "Refugees," www.yahoodi.com/peace/refugees.html.

———, "Yassir Arafat," www.yahoodi.com/peace/arafat.html.

Paul Reynolds, "Arafat: The Great Survivor," British Broadcasting Company, May 2, 2002. http://news.bbc.co.uk/1/hi/world/middle_east/1962733.stm.

Charles E. Schumer, "Hamas: The Organization, Goals, and Tactics of a

Militant Palestinian Organization," *Intelligence Resource Program*, October 14, 1993. www.fas.org/irp/crs/931014-hamas.htm.

Jami Tarabay, "Prominent Palestinians Condemn Suicide Bombings," 2002. www.converge.org/nz/pma/cra0575.htm.

Scott Weinsten, "Diaries: Sharon's Pattern of Provocation," *Electronic Intifada*, December 26, 2003. http://electronicintifada.net/v2/article2302.shtml.

Kathryn Westcott, "Who Are Hamas?" British Broadcasting Company, October 19, 2000. http://news.bbc.co.uk/1/hi/world/middle_east/978626.stm.

INDEX

PICTURE CREDITS

Cover photo: Andrea Comas/Reuters/Landov

AP/Wide World Photos, 25, 52

Ammar Awad/Reuters/Landov, 44, 47, 51, 69

Alaa Badarneh/EPA/Landov, 75

© Bettmann/CORBIS, 38

Central State Archive of Film, Photo, and Phonographic Documents, courtesy of USHMM Photo Archives, 22

Eric Gaillard/Reuters/Landov, 87

© Getty Images, 40

Abed Al-Hafiz Hashlamoun/EPA/Landov, 73

Gary Hershorn/Reuters/Landov, 42

Jim Holander/EPA/Landov, 85

Hulton/Archive by Getty Images, 15, 16, 18, 23, 26, 29, 32, 37

Ahmed Jadallah/Reuters/Landov, 63, 64

Ali Jarekji/Reuters/Landov, 39

Reinhard Krause/Reuters/Landov, 61, 79

Gil Cohen Magen/Reuters/Landov, 56

Abed Omar Qusini/Reuters/Landov, 76-77

Mohammed Saber/EPA/Landov, 11, 71

Mohammed Salem/Reuters/Landov, 59

Suhaib Salem/Reuters/Landov, 60, 88, 90

Jihad Seqlawi/AFP/Getty Images, 84

Mario Tama/Getty Images, 92

Goran Tomasevic/Reuters/Landov, 70

Valdrin Xhemaj/EPA/Landov, 81

Steve Zmina, 49

ABOUT THE AUTHOR

Anne Wallace Sharp is the author of one book of adult nonfiction, *Gifts*, a compilation of stories about hospice patients; and several children's books, including *Daring Women Pirates* and seven previous titles for Lucent Books. In addition, she has written numerous magazine articles for both the adult and juvenile markets. A retired registered nurse, Sharp has a degree in history. Her other interests include reading, traveling, and spending time with her two grandchildren, Jacob and Nicole. Sharp lives in Beavercreek, Ohio.